P9-DDH-553

NATIVE TRIBES OF NORTH AMERICA

NATIVE TRIBES OF THE
# GREAT BASIN AND PLATEAU

Michael Johnson
& Duncan Clarke

WORLD ALMANAC® LIBRARY

Library of Congress Cataloging-in-Publication Data

Johnson, Michael, 1937 Apr. 22-
   Native tribes of the Great Basin and Plateau / by Michael Johnson and Duncan Clarke.
      p. cm. — (Native tribes of North America)
   Summary: An introduction to the history, culture, and people of the many Indian tribes that inhabited the region of the present states of Utah
and Nevada and the mountainous area of the northwest United States and southern British Columbia in Canada.
   Includes bibliographical references and index.
   ISBN 0-8368-5610-4 (lib. bdg.)
   1. Indians of North America—Great Basin—History—Juvenile literature.   2. Indians of North America—Great Basin—Social life and customs—Juvenile
literature.   3. Indians of North America—Northwest, Pacific—History—Juvenile literature.   4. Indians of North America—Northwest, Pacific—Social life
and customs—Juvenile literature.   [1. Indians of North America—Great Basin.   2. Indians of North America—Northwest, Pacific.] I. Clarke, Duncan,
1962-.   II. Title.
   E78.G67J65   2004
   979.004'97—dc22
                                                                                                                        2003060452

This edition copyright © 2004 by World Almanac® Library. Original copyright © 2004 Compendium Publishing Limited.

This North American edition first published in 2004 by
**World Almanac® Library**
330 West Olive Street, Suite 100
Milwaukee, WI 53212 USA

For Compendium Publishing
Contributors: Michael Johnson and Duncan Clarke
Editor: Michael Burke
Picture research: Michael Johnson, and Simon Forty
Design: Tony Stocks/Compendium Design
Maps: Mark Franklin

World Almanac® Library editor: Gini Holland
World Almanac® Library graphic designer: Steve Schraenkler

Picture credits

All artwork (other than maps) reproduced by kind permission of Richard Hook. All photographs are by Michael Johnson or supplied from his
collection unless credited otherwise below. Particular thanks are due to the staff of Royal Albert Memorial Museum and Art Gallery, Exeter, Devon,
U.K., for assistance and access to its exhibits, archives, and excellent collections, and to Bill Yenne for material of his own and from his collection.
Much of the material in this book appeared as part of *The Encyclopedia of Native Tribes of North America* by M. J. Johnson and R. Hook, published
by Compendium Publishing Ltd. in 2001.

Richard Green Collection (photography by Simon Clay): p. 41; Werner Forman Archive: p. 6; Santa Fe Railway: p. 49; Courtesy Ian West: p. 56; Bill
Yenne: pp. 20, 22 (below), 26, 37, 39, 40.

Printed in the United States of America

1 2 3 4 5 6 7 8 9 08 07 06 05 04

Cover: Alby and Hattie (Hatty) Shawaway, Yakima Indians, c. 1950, wearing beaded costume partly influenced by Plains Indians.

Previous page: Nez Perce beaded flat bag.

# Contents

# Introduction

Below: **A Kutenai group at the turn of the century. The Kutenai are believed to have once lived on the northern Great Plains, but either migrated or were forced— probably by the Blackfeet— across the Rocky Mountains into what is now southeastern British Columbia.**

For thousands of years, the people known today as Native Americans or American Indians have inhabited the whole of the Americas, from Alaska to the southernmost tip of South America. Most scholars and anthropologists think that the ancestors of Native peoples came to the Americas from Asia over a land mass connecting Siberia and Alaska. These first Americans may have arrived as long as 30,000 years ago, although most historians estimate that this migration took place 15,000 years ago.

According to this theory, Paleo-Indians (*paleo*, from a Greek word meaning "ancient") migrated over many years down through an ice-free corridor in North America, spreading out from west to east and southward into Central and South America. In time, they inhabited the entire Western Hemisphere from north to south. Their descendants became the many diverse Native peoples encountered by European explorers and settlers.

## "INDIANS" VS. "NATIVE AMERICANS"

Christopher Columbus is said to have "discovered" the Americas in 1492. But did he? Columbus was not the first European to visit what became known as the New World; Viking mariners had sailed to Greenland and Newfoundland almost five hundred years before and even founded short-lived colonies. Using the word "discovered" also ignores the fact that North America was already inhabited by Native civilizations whose ancestors had "discovered" the Americas for themselves.

When Columbus landed on an island he called San Salvador (Spanish for "Holy Savior"), he thought he had reached China or Japan. He had sailed west intending to get to the East—to Asia, or the fabled "Indies," as it was often called by Europeans of the time. Although he landed in the Bahamas, Columbus never really gave up on the idea that he had made it to the Indies. Thus when Native people first encountered Columbus and his men in the islands off Florida, the lost explorer called them "Indians." The original names that each tribal group had already given to themselves usually translate into English as "the people" or "human beings." Today, some Native people of North

America prefer to be called "American Indians," while others prefer "Native Americans." In this book, Native peoples will be referred to by their tribal names or, in more general cases, as "Indians."

Today's Indians are descended from cultures of great historical depth, diversity, and complexity. Their ancient ancestors, the Paleo-Indians, developed beliefs and behavior patterns that enabled them to survive in unpredictable and often harsh environments. These early hunter-gatherers had a close relationship with the land and a sense of absolute and eternal belonging to it. To them, everything in their world—trees, mountains, rivers, sky, animals, rock formations—had "spirit power," which they respected and placated through prayers and rituals in order to ensure their survival. These beliefs evolved over time into a fascinating and diverse series of creation stories, trickster tales, songs, prayers, and rituals passed down to and practiced by tribes throughout North America. Although many Indians today practice Christianity and other religions as well, many of their traditional songs, stories, dances, and other practices survive, on reservations and in areas where substantial tribal groups still live.

## A CONTINENT OF CULTURES

Long before the Europeans arrived, important Indian cultures had already developed and disappeared. The ancient Adena and Hopewell people, for example, built a number of extraordinary burial mounds, and later even large towns, some of whose remains can still be seen at sites in the Midwest and South. These cultures were themselves gradually influenced by Mesoamerican (pre-Columbian Mexican and Central American) farming cultures based on growing maize (Indian corn), beans, and squash. They became the Mississippian culture from 700 A.D. The great spread of language groups across the North American continent also points to a rich Indian history of continual movement, invasion, migration, and conquest that took place long before European contact.

By the time the first European explorers and colonists set foot in North America, Indians had settled across the vast continent into different tribal groups and cultures that were active, energetic, and continually changing. American Indians were skilled in exploiting their particular

## U.S. INDIAN POPULATION

There is no record of the number of Indians living north of the Rio Grande before Europeans came. A conservative estimate of Indian population made by ethnographer James Mooney is about 1,250,000 for the late sixteenth century, before the founding of Jamestown and Plymouth. Others have suggested figures as high as six million, although two to three million might be more realistic. The highest concentrations of people were in the coastal regions: the Atlantic slope in the East, along the Gulf of Mexico in the South, and in California in the West. Indians living in these areas also suffered the most from European diseases and from conflict with European colonists. Population figures for the twentieth century vary considerably, due mainly to U.S. government criteria used to determine who is or is not an Indian. Also, the U.S. Bureau of Indian Affairs (BIA), the official bureaucracy in charge of the remaining Indian lands and federal services to Indians, has few relations with Indians in certain states. Thus the BIA's population figures tend to be lower than those reported by the U.S. Census. In 1950 the BIA reported 396,000 enrolled Indians, of whom 245,000 were resident on reservations. The U.S. Census reported 827,108 Indians in 1970 and 1,418,195 in 1980. Census 2000 recorded 2,409,578 respondents who reported as American Indian or Alaskan Native only and identified a single tribe of origin.

Above: **The hostile environment of the Great Basin includes mountain and desert areas.**

## CENSUS 2000 FIGURES

Wherever possible U.S. Census 2000 figures are supplied with each entry showing the number of people who identified that they were American Indian or Alaskan Native and members of only one tribe. Other people reported as American Indian or Alaskan Native in combination with one or more other races (defined in the census as including white, black or African-American, Native Hawaiian, and other Pacific Islander) and showing more than one tribe of origin are identified as "part...." Reporting variables mean that some of the totals published here may not be the precise sum of the individual elements.

environments in a multitude of ways developed over time. They were also good at incorporating new methods and technologies from other peoples. When Europeans came, many Indians adapted European technology to their own way of life, incorporating, for example, the horse, the rifle, money, beads, fabric, steel implements, and European-style agriculture into their own traditional cultures. In many cases, however, the benefits of European influence were eventually overshadowed by the displacement or outright destruction of traditional Native life.

## WHAT THIS BOOK COVERS

The purpose of this book is to give some relevant facts about the main tribes native to the Great Basin and Plateau. There are brief historical sketches of the tribes, descriptions of tribal language relationships and groups, and accounts of traditional cultures, tribal locations, and populations in early and recent times. Interaction with invading Europeans is shown in the trade, wars, treaties, and eventual Indian removal to lands whose boundaries served more to keep Indians in than to keep white settlers out. Today's political boundaries were not recognized by Indians on their original lands: Their borders were the shifting lines of hunting, gathering, and farming areas used and fought over by different tribes. For ease of reference, however, tribal locations given here refer to modern American and Canadian place names.

## THE GREAT BASIN

The Indians who lived in the vast area of present-day Nevada, Utah, the western parts of Colorado and Wyoming, southern Idaho, and adjacent parts of Oregon and California, sharing a similar lifestyle, formed the Great Basin cultural area. The area is bounded by the Snake River in the north and reaches down almost to the Colorado River in the south, totaling roughly 400,000 square miles (1,036,000 square kilometers). The Indians of the area belong mainly to the old Shoshonean language family (now designated as the Uto-Aztecan family), specifically to the Numic division, except for the Washoe, whose distant relatives are the Hokans of California. The boundaries between tribes were fluid, with movement and marriage common between tribes.

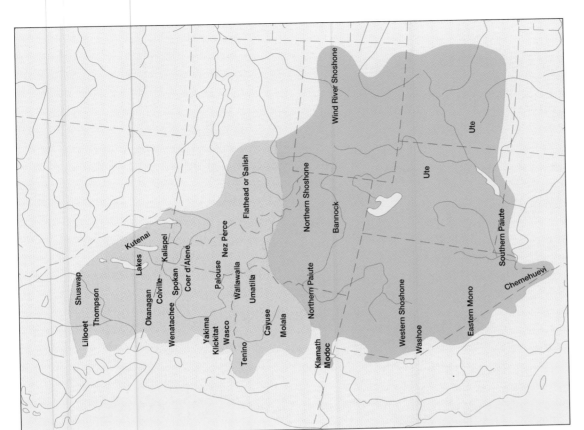

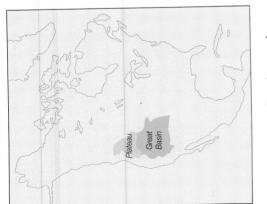

The Great Basin region is mostly high desert and semidesert where sparse vegetation, sagebrush, and extremely meager grassland are typical, though there are also mountains reaching over 12,000 feet (3,660 meters), and both saltwater and freshwater lakes. In the east, canyons and valleys support woodlands and bush, dotted with occasional marshy patches. Animal resources are sparse: The main game animals were squirrels, rabbits, and fish, with occasional antelope, deer, and bison; even gophers and grasshoppers were eaten. Seeds, roots, and berries supplied up to three quarters of Great Basin people's food supplies. The most important of these were the piñon nut and the acorn harvests from which mush, flour, and cakes could be made. Only a few southern groups practiced a limited form of farming, growing small amounts of corn, beans, and squash. For most of the Indians of the Great Basin, the daily routine revolved around the quest to gather food in a largely inhospitable and demanding climate that regularly produced extremes of both heat and cold.

Because of this hostile environment, much of the

**Above:** The area covered in this book. The Great Basin includes most of the present states of Utah and Nevada. The Plateau is the mountainous area of the northwestern United States and southern British Columbia, Canada.

# THE HORSE AND THE INDIANS OF THE PLATEAU

The horse reached the Umatilla in Oregon as early as 1739, moving north among the Indians of the Continental Divide. Mobility provided by the horse allowed Indians to conduct yearly hunts and raids on the plains of Montana. Hence—as illustrated in this image of a Nez Perce man, c. 1877—the material culture and dress of the Plateau show similarities born of friendly trade relations with the Crow: horse collars, gun cases, bandolier bags, and blanket strips bore similar beaded designs, such as hourglass shapes, isosceles triangles, and crosses, and similarly sophisticated use of colors, sewn onto hide or cloth in a flat mosaic form. Nez Perce warriors wore both upright and flared bonnets; a style intermediate between the two is illustrated. The Nez Perce were famous for these Appaloosa horses.

Great Basin was among the last areas of the United States to be taken over by non-Natives. The area became known to the Spanish in the late eighteenth century, and to Americans after the explorations of Jedediah Smith (c. 1824–31) and John C. Frémont (1843–44).

White settlement was limited, however, as most immigrant parties were just crossing the Great Basin on their way to California. Consequently, the Indians did not immediately suffer removal as elsewhere, but nevertheless their lifestyle was dramatically affected within a few years. Small numbers of ranchers and farmers soon degraded the area's fragile ecology: Within a short period, hunger and exposure to new diseases had caused a drastic population decline.

After 1850, reservations were established. Over the following century, generally harsh, inconsistent government policies deprived the surviving peoples of much of their land and economic prospects. Since the 1960s, successful land claims and increased tribal self-determination, combined with federal support, have assisted some groups and eased the worst hardships. Unemployment and inadequate social facilities remain major problems throughout the area, however.

## THE PLATEAU

The Indians who lived in parts of the present states of Idaho, Washington, Oregon, parts of adjacent states, and of British Columbia in Canada constituted a culture area

Above: Flathead, or Kutenai, beaded vest from Montana, c. 1890. European-style clothes, vests, gloves, gauntlets, and pants were adopted by Indians during the nineteenth century but decorated in their own unique way.

Above and Below: **Two Plateau beaded women's flat bags, probably Yakima (above) and Klikitat (below), c. 1900. These probably derive from earlier corn husk bags and were carried by women at celebrations.**

now known as the Plateau. It takes in around 240,000 square miles (621,000 sq km) east of the Coast Range and Cascade Mountains, drained by two major river systems, the Columbia and the Fraser. The land ranges from heavily forested areas in the north through barren uplands, mountains with patches of forest and lakes, to a semiarid desert in the south.

Inland, fish (particularly salmon) were of vital importance in the diet of most Plateau groups. They also hunted game that included deer, elk, mountain sheep, bear, rabbit, and squirrels, while women gathered numerous plant foods such as camas, cous (or cowish) root, and many types of berries. Often they had to move over quite long distances within their territory to take best advantage of the changing food supplies available at different times of the year. During the hot summers, Plateau Indians lived in conical or gable pole structures covered with brush or cattail mats; later, Plains-type tipis became common. In the winter, they built circular lodges sunk in the ground about 5 feet (1.5 m) deep, roofed over with grass, brush, or earth over planks.

Religion in the Plateau involved relationships between people and the spirits believed to live in natural things, including features of the landscape as well as animals and plants. People were thought to gain their powers and skills from these individual guiding spirits, with shamans and other leaders having particularly powerful spirit helpers.

Aside from the linguistically distinct Kutenai people, most Plateau tribes spoke dialects of the Sahaptian or interior Salishan languages.

The horse, originally acquired from the Spanish, reached the Umatilla in Oregon as early as 1739, moving north among the Indians of the Continental Divide. As well as extending the range of annual migrations and allowing larger quantities of dried foods to be transported and traded, the mobility provided by the horse allowed yearly hunting and raiding as far east as the plains of Montana. The Nez Perce, in particular, developed strong trade relations with the Crow and Flathead peoples. In later days, the bark, grass, and fur outfits of the Plateau increasingly gave way to skin tunics for men and dresses for women that superficially

# TRIBAL NAMES

| Tribe | Meaning of name |
|---|---|
| Bannock | English name |
| Cayuse | – |
| Chelan | – |
| Coeur d'Alene | French—awl heart |
| Colville | English name |
| Flathead or Salish | people |
| Kalispel | camas (plant) |
| Klamath | people |
| Klikitat | beyond |
| Kutenai | division name |
| Lillooet | wild onion |
| Methow | – |
| Modoc | southerners |
| Molala | place name |
| Mono | – |
| Nez Perce | French—pierced noses |
| Okanagan | place name |

| Tribe | Meaning of name |
|---|---|
| Paiute | Spanish name |
| Palouse | – |
| Salish | people |
| Sanpoil and Nespelem | – |
| Senijextee | lake people |
| Shoshone | – |
| Shuswap | – |
| Sinkiuse | band name |
| Spokan | sun people |
| Tenino | – |
| Thompson | English name |
| Umatilla | – |
| Ute | Spanish name |
| Wailatpuan | – |
| Walla Walla | – |
| Wenatchi | little river |
| Yakima | place name |
|  | runaway |

Above: Tribal names are—for the most part—not the old names by which the Indians knew themselves. Many names translate simply as "real men" or "original people." The common, popular, modern names used are derived from various sources. Some are from Native terms, either by the people for themselves or names applied by neighbors or enemies, or corruptions of these terms. Some tribal names are anglicized (made English) forms of translated Native names; others are from French or Spanish sources. We use the tribal names most commonly encountered in history and literature, although it should be noted that some modern Indian groups have successfully reintroduced their own names into current usage.

resembled Plains attire, and there were similarities in decoration of ceremonial dress as well. Many tribes produced fine basketry.

By the time Lewis and Clark reached the plateau in 1804–06, the advance spread of imported diseases such as smallpox had already caused a drastic decline in population among many tribes. The arrival of missionaries and traders transformed Native life in the area by the 1840s, and a number of conflicts occurred between white intruders and the Cayuse, Yakima, Nez Perce, and Palouse. Although most of the larger inland Salish and Sahaptian tribes survived the invasion, smaller western groups suffered greatly, particularly the Cayuse, Molala, and groups close to the Columbia River. Both armed resistance (particularly among the Yakima in the 1850s) and a famous flight to Canada by the Nez Perce in the 1870s proved futile. Over the following century, the surviving Plateau Indians were grouped onto reservations. Their culture was badly eroded by missionaries and government officials, and opportunities for education and economic progress were very limited. Since the 1960s, there have been some improvements and a greater pride in Indian identity and heritage, but, despite some progress in areas such as logging, fishing, gaming, and mineral rights, many problems remain.

# FLATHEAD OR SALISH

The Flatheads were the easternmost Salishan tribe, living in western Montana in the valleys between the Rocky Mountains and the Bitterroot Range. They now mostly prefer to be known as Salish, although the Salishan language family also includes numerous other groups, such as the Shuswap, Okanagan, Wenatchi, Sanpoil, Kalispel, Coeur d'Alene, Columbia, Thompson, Fraser, Lillooet, and Spokan. These people are together known to scholars as Interior Salish, to distinguish them from the better known but culturally unrelated Coast Salish of the Northwest Coast.

Below: Indian girls of the Flathead Reservation, Montana, 1907, riding ponies with beaded saddles upon which great skill and time has been spent. The girls' ponies are adorned with a variety of Plains and Plateau finery.

Among several of these Interior Salish peoples in the nineteenth century, it was customary for mothers to reshape the head of their baby by binding it tightly while the skull was still soft in the first few months after birth to compress it against a cedar board. The aim was to create a smooth, "flat" profile line down from the forehead to the nose. Although European missionaries regarded this process as barbaric, it was in fact harmless and caused no pain to the child. There is some confusion in the early contact sources as to precisely which groups followed this distinctive practice, but most references today suggest that, ironically, the so-called Flatheads were not among them. Some argue that, rather than referring to the flat forehead created by the technique, the name was a local Indian term that distinguished this group from their neighbors, whose use of cranial deformation gave them pointed heads! In any event, the group called themselves *Se'lic*, meaning "people."

The Interior Salish acquired horses in about 1700 from nearby groups of Plains Indians. Over the following century, as they adapted to a life of buffalo raiding on the flatlands and the larger band organization it required, their culture and lifestyle increasingly came to resemble that of Plains peoples. On the Plains they were friendly with most groups they met, with the exception of the Blackfeet, with whom they fought a number of battles.

Their contacts with the Lewis and Clark expedition in 1805 were their first encounter with non-Native people. They were friendly and hospitable, trading with and supplying food to their visitors. Clark records on October 21, 1805, "J. Collins presented us with verry good beer made of the Pa-shi-co-quar-mash [camass] bread, which bread is the remains of what was laid in as a part of

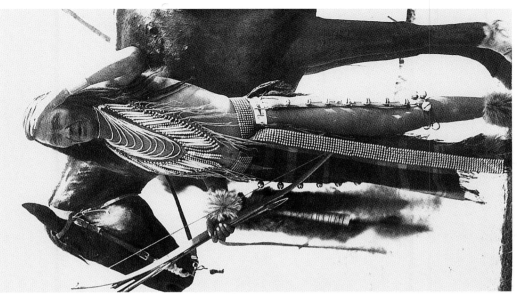

Below: Flathead man, c. 1907, holding a bow and arrows. His belt appears to be decorated with brass studs. This photograph was taken on the Flathead Reservation, Montana.

Below: Flathead singers, c. 1907. With the increasing social function of Plains/Plateau ceremonialism early in the last century, specialist "singing" groups (never called "drummers") provided accompanying songs for Owl, Grass, Tea, and Rabbit Dances. Western bass drums, more reliable in sound, often replaced Native drums. Each "singer" used a single drumstick, and for certain dances performers knelt around the drum.

our Stores of Provisions, at the first flat heads or Cho-pun-nish Nation at the head of the Kosskoske river." When they first met in September, Clark recorded that the Flathead party at Clark's River had approximately 400 people, including 80 men. The Flatheads showed their welcome toward the men of the expedition by wrapping white robes on the men's shoulders and smoking peace pipes with them, prompting Lewis and Clark to decide that the exploration party should encamp with the Flatheads for the night. The most noticeable initial impression they made, according to the journals of various expedition members, was through their language, which was described as a gurgling in the throat unlike any Native American speech they had encountered so far.

Interestingly, some Indian recollections of the historic meeting have also survived. Among them is this account: "The Flathead Indians were camping at Ross's Hole, or Ross's fork, at the head of the Bitterroot valley, when one day the old chief, Three Eagles, the father of Chief Victor and grandfather of Charlot, left the camp to go scouting the country, fearing there might be some Indian enemies around with the intent to steal horses, as it was done then very frequently. He saw at a distance Lewis and Clark's party, about twenty men, each man leading two pack horses, except two, who were riding ahead, who were Lewis and Clark. . . . When the two leaders of the party, coming to the Indian camp, showed friendship to the Indians, there was a universal shaking of hands. The chief then gave orders to the Indians to bring in the best buffalo hides, one for each man to sit on, and the best buffalo robes also, one for each man to use as a blanket." (Francois Saxa's account of the story of Agnes, Chief Victor's widow, reported by Jerome D'Aste, S. J.)

Writing in 1806, Meriwether Lewis provided a detailed and fascinating account of the clothing worn by the Flatheads. Lewis recorded that male dress was a "small robe" tied at the shoulder with a string across the chest, which could be worn to cover one or both arms. It reached down to the thighs but left the shoulders and back bare. Lewis noted, "a mat is sometimes temporarily thrown over the sholders to protect them from rain," but the men wore no other article of clothing regardless of the season. He observed that "they are very fond of the dress of the

Below: Louis Charlemain (He Rolls Around), a Flathead man with his daughters, c. 1907. He is holding a Civil War bayonet.

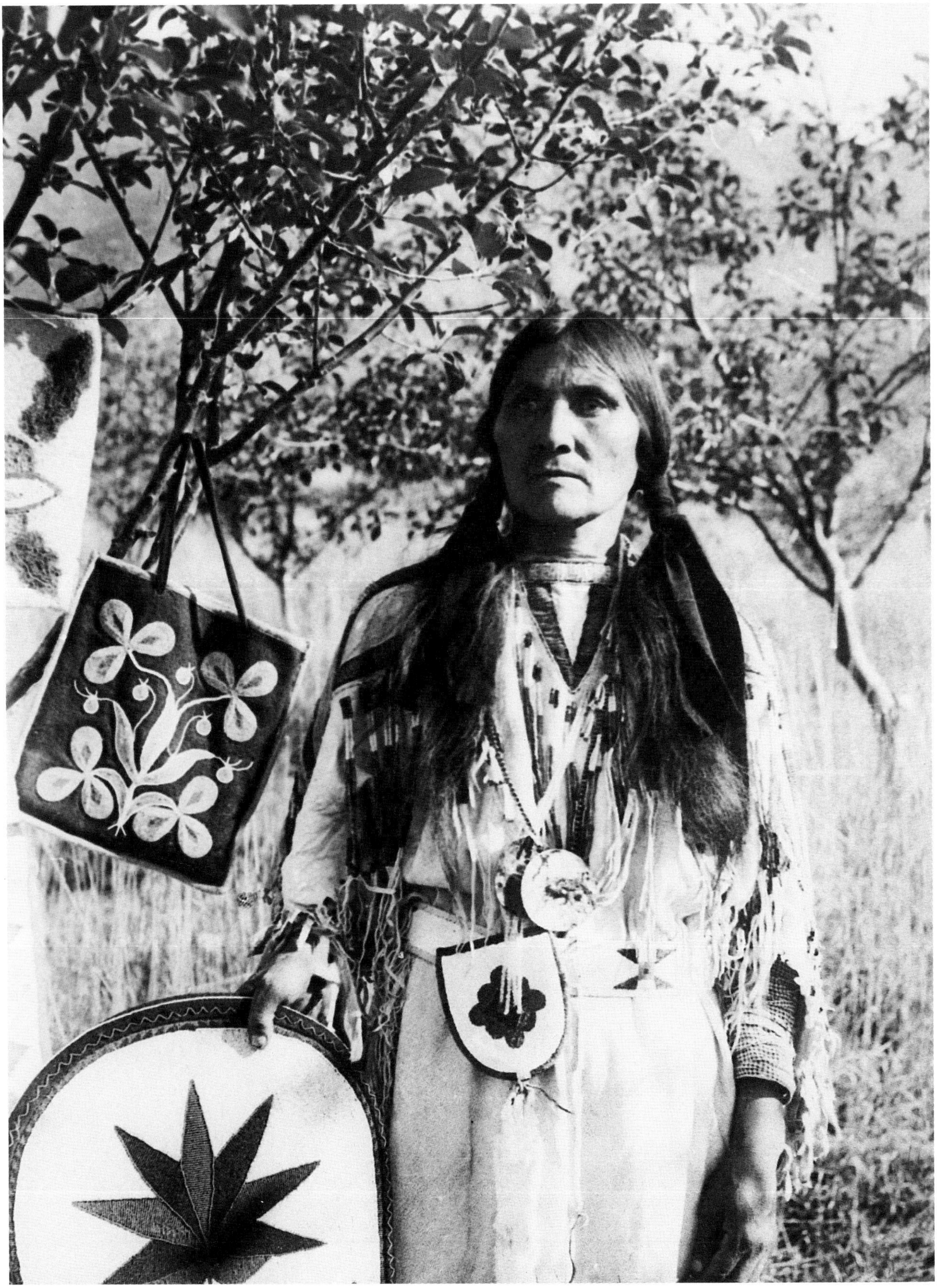

whites, which they wear in a similar manner when they can obtain them, except the shoe which I have never seen woarn by any of them." As for the women, Lewis recorded, "The dress of the women consists of a robe, tissue, and sometimes when the weather is uncommonly cold, a vest." The vest was similar to a man's robe except that it did not reach lower than the waist.

Lewis went on to note that "the most esteemed and valuable of these robes are made of strips of the skins of the Sea Otter net together with the bark of the white cedar or silk grass," which "make a warm and soft covering." Other examples used beaver or raccoon fur. Women wore a skirtlike cloth from the waist to the knees. It was made from "a tissue of white cedar bark, bruised or broken into small shreds, which are interwoven." Turning to jewelry, he wrote that "the favorite ornament of both sexes are the common coarse blue and white beads which the men wear tightly wound around their wrists and ankles many times," making a solid band three inches or more thick. Men also wore beads loosely around their necks or hanging from pierced noses or ears, but women never pierced their noses. Lewis also observed that "the men sometimes wear collars of bear claws, and the women and children the tusks of the Elk variously arranged on their necks arms &c."

Like other Interior Salish peoples, the women of the Flathead group made a wide range of beautiful coiled grass baskets. Large baskets were made for use as packs transporting household goods and dried foods as the band traveled around their territory. Smaller ones served as collecting bowls for berries, roots, and seeds. Rectangular baskets about twenty-four inches long were made as cradles for infants. Many of these were fitted with wooden hoops to support a sunshade. Woven from squaw grass and other local grasses, the baskets' natural tan color formed a background for designs such as zigzags, lozenges, abstract plant shapes, and, in a few examples, images of people and horses using fibers dyed black or red with plant dyes. Today only a few

Right and Below: Flathead man "Loma" photographed in Montana, c. 1907. Clearly a man of prestige, he wears (below) a "straight-up eaglefeather bonnet," with quill-decorated spines, a loop necklace, trade blanket leggings with beaded panels, beaded moccasins, and belt. At right he has his hair in braids and wears a shirt decorated with strips of floral beadwork. His photographer is unknown, but was possibly Edward H. Boos, examples of whose work are in the collections of the Denver Public Library, Western History Department, and the Birmingham Reference Library, England.

women still have the skills to keep these ancient traditions alive, and baskets collected in the nineteenth and early twentieth century are highly valued museum pieces.

During the first half of the nineteenth century, the Flatheads were involved in the fur trade, and relations with whites were still generally friendly. As part of these links, some Flatheads adopted aspects of the Catholic faith through contacts with Iroquois fur traders who had been converted in contact with the Hudson's Bay Company. They sent various delegations to the Jesuits at St. Louis asking for a missionary priest, and in 1840 the well-known missionary father Pierre De Smet was sent. In 1841, he founded the mission of St. Mary on the Bitterroot River. Nine years later this had to be abandoned because of Blackfeet attacks, but the new mission of St. Ignatius that he established south of Flathead Lake remains in operation today.

Father De Smet was also interested in Indian art, and one of his ledgers has since provided a vital early record of the meanings associated with symbols found in rock art, painted robes, beadwork, and other art forms throughout the region. De Smet made this record through a series of interviews with a Flathead chief called Five Crows, also known by his adopted Christian name of Ambrose. In the ledger, which has recently been analyzed by the archaeologist Dr. James Keyser, Five Crows drew numerous small pictures of battles made up of about one hundred symbols, each of which he explained to De Smet. For instance, a bag surrounded by tiny lightning bolts is interpreted as a medicine bundle that gave its owner access to supernatural power. Many of these symbols are archaic motifs shared throughout large areas of North America, and the Five Crows/De Smet ledger, along with a handful of other examples, will be vital in deepening understanding of Native American art and culture.

Although the Salish signed a treaty with the U.S. government in 1855 and were assigned a reservation around Flathead Lake, Montana, many were able to continue living without being confined until the

Right: Pierre Paul, Flathead Indian, c. 1907, wearing the earrings and multiple strands of beads preferred by Flathead men.

1870s, and the last band, led by Charlot, held out in the Bitterroot Mountains until 1891. On the Flathead Reservation, the Salish were ultimately combined with part of the Spokan, some Lower Kalispel, most of the Upper Kalispel or Pend d'Oreilles, and some Kutenai. The reservation covers 1,244,000 acres (503,447 square hectares), but today around half the land and 80 percent of the population is non-Indian. The true Flatheads were usually reported to number around 600; in 1909, 598. The population of the whole "Confederated Salish-Kutenai" of the Flathead Reservation was given as 3,085 in 1937; 3,630 in 1945; and 5,937 in 1980. Census 2000 recorded 3,310 Salish and a further 1,429 part Salish, the figures for the "Salish and Kootenai" being 3,464 and 736.

The tribe today receives an income of $10 million per year from an annual lease on the Kerr Dam on the Lower Flathead River, and is due to become owners of the license in 2015. Other sources of income include the KwataqNuk tourist resort on Flathead Lake, and some ownership of local forestry and ranching projects. Despite these developments, however, unemployment and social problems remain high. A health care agreement with the federal government in 1994 added $12 million annually to the tribal budget. The two Eagle River High Schools and the Salish-Kootenai College were founded during the 1970s. The Arlee powwow is held in July, and other cultural events are expressions of the Flatheads' continuing cohesion as an Indian people.

Below: A colorful roadside advertisement for one example of the Flathead tourist industry. The "Discount cigarettes" promoted here tend to draw customers because Native tribal stores are not subject to the same high tax on cigarettes that non-Indian stores must charge.

A tribe of Indians speaking a language that is thought to be unrelated to those of other Indian peoples. Their own name was San'ka, which means "people of the waters." The Kutenai are believed to have once lived on the northern Great Plains, but later to have either migrated or been forced, probably by the Blackfeet, across the Rocky Mountains into what is now southeastern British Columbia. Perhaps as a result of this movement they split into an upper and a lower division. The Upper Kutenai pushed south into present Montana on the Tobacco Plains and were influenced by the horse-buffalo Plains Indian culture complex, as well as retaining some of their own Plains origins. They used horses for transportation and as a source of wealth, and adopted the Sun Dance and material culture and costume associated with the northern Plains Indians. By comparison, the Lower Kutenai were semi-nomadic, of the true Plateau culture, subsisting on fish, roots, and game, and are famous for their remarkable canoe. The Lower Kutenai were also known as the Arcplat, or Flatbow, Indians, a name inspired by the shape of Kootenay Lake. In precontact times they perhaps numbered 2,000, but only 500 or so by 1855.

Like other Indian peoples of the Plateau, the Kutenai believed that each natural object had a spirit, and that there was an overall master spirit, which was sometimes associated with the sun. Edward S. Curtis, who photographed many western Indians in the late nineteenth and early twentieth century, noted that at the end of the winter, the Kutenai performed a rite called Kankonohl for the purpose of securing the continued favor of a god, who had influence over game animals and the power to grant wealth. As adolescents, both boys and girls would go on vision quests where they sought the help of a guardian spirit. Shamans, who could be male or female, acquired additional and more powerful spirit guides through dreams, whom they believed would allow them to cure the sick and foretell the future. There were three religious societies: the Crazy Dogs, the Crazy Owls, and Shamans. Among

Below: The Kutenai account for about a quarter of the Confederated Salish-Kutenai.

Below: "Sturgeon nose" canoes were characteristic of the Kutenai and Shuswap. The Kutenai canoe, unique to this group, was made from a single piece of white pine bark that was laid, smooth side out, over a frame of cedar strips and maple ribs. Either cedar root or wild cherry bark was used for binding, and pitch from the ponderosa pine or Douglas fir provided caulking materials to seal joints and knotholes. It is still regarded as one of the finest Native American canoe types.

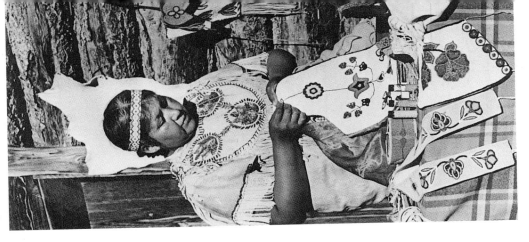

Below: Margaret Tenasse, Kootenay (Kutenai) and examples of her beadwork at her home near Windermere, British Columbia, c. 1945. Before the French began calling them the Kutenai, they called themselves the Ksunka, or "People of the Standing Arrow." Arrows represent strength, unity, and dexterity— three qualities which they honored and strived to represent.

Upper Kutenai it was a council of shamans that elected the band chief, who was assisted by a war chief and a hunting chief. When leadership (and negotiations with whites) became more crucial during the nineteenth century, the chieftaincy became hereditary, although most decisions were still reached by group consensus.

Among Kutenai myths is the story of the frog that raced and outwitted the antelope, a local version of the tale of the tortoise and the hare. Upper Kutenai groups wore Plains-style clothing, while Lower Kutenai people dressed in clothes made from bark, hemp, and matting. In addition to baskets they made carved wooden bowls, clay pots, and stone pipes. The Kutenai were not notably warlike, although they did fight occasional small-scale conflicts with the Blackfeet, Assiniboine, and Cree.

Most of the Upper Kutenai, originally from around Jennings and Libby, Montana, under the name Dayton-Elmo band, joined the Flathead and their associates on the Flathead (Jocko) Agency; the Lower Kutenai, with additions from the Tobacco Plains band, obtained reserves in British Columbia around Creston, Windermere, and Cranbrook, and also near Bonners Ferry, Idaho. In 1907, 573 Kutenai were recorded in Montana and 549 in British Columbia. The Bonners Ferry group reported 106 in 1945, and 115 in 1982.

The Kutenai perhaps constitute a quarter of the present, so-called Confederated Salish-Kutenai, numbering 3,225 in 1985, but many now live off the reservation. Also in 2000 are reported 618 "Kootenai." In 1970, the Canadian Kutenai at Columbia Lake, Lower Kootenay, St. Mary's, and Tobacco Plains numbered 446. All four Canadian bands are affiliated to the Ktunaxa/Kinbasket Tribal Council, and with very small allocations of land obtain a limited income from such activities as campsites, logging, and tourist ranches. There are art and craft activities and a museum on the land of the St. Mary's Band. On the Kutenai Reservation at Bonners Ferry there are a fish hatchery, craft shop, and motel. The cultural traditions, language, and religion of the Kutenai seem to have survived better on the Idaho reservation than on the Reservation in Montana.

MONO

Below: Owens Valley Paiute (Eastern Mono). Rush mat conical dwelling, with child in cradleboard, c. 1890.

# EASTERN MONO or OWENS VALLEY PAIUTE

A branch of the Uto-Aztecan family closely connected linguistically with the Northern Paiute, who occupied the valley of the Owens River parallel with the southern Sierra Nevada Mountains, Inyo County, California. A transitional group (combining aspects of Great Basin cultural practices with other features more closely related to their California neighbors), they are noted for their early use of irrigation techniques, including temporary dams and the diversion of small feeder streams to provide a regular flow of water to their patches of wild roots and seed plants. A specific individual was chosen to be responsible for each area to be irrigated, though communal assistance was provided for the actual work. Unlike most other Great Basin peoples, the Owens Valley Paiutes lived in semipermanent village-like camps to which the same group of families would return each year at the appropriate season. Neighboring villages cooperated on irrigation projects, large hunts, and important funerals. People married between the villages.

The Owens Valley Paiute were defeated by incoming whites in 1863. After several years of resistance, they scattered to the small towns and farms as laborers. Reservations were not established until the twentieth century; the descendants of the Owens Valley Paiute are at Benton (in Mono County, with the Paiute), Bishop, Big Pine, Independence, Lone Pine (with the Panamint), and throughout Inyo County. They number perhaps 1,800 including the

Western Mono (Monache) and Panamint, the three being almost indistinguishable from one another. In 1991, there were 2,266 Owens Valley Paiutes, about 950 of them on the reservations mentioned above.

## WESTERN MONO or MONACHE

A group of six small Shoshonean (Numic) Uto-Aztecan speaking tribes related to the Owens Valley and Northern Paiute. They were more Californian in culture than Great Basin, since they lived on the west slope of the Sierra Nevada on the upper reaches of the San Joaquin (North Fork), Kings, and Kaweah rivers in California, where they shared a general culture with the neighboring Yokuts. Mono groups included the North Fork, Wobonuch, Entimbich, Michahay, Waksachi, and Patwisha. Their subsistence depended on hunting, fishing, and gathering. Acorns were their most important source of nourishment, supplemented by roots, seeds, and berries, together with fish and small game.

The Mono traded products such as obsidian and rabbit skins with the nearby Yokuts and with the Owens Valley Paiute to the east of the mountains. They used log rafts to cross major rivers and had waterproof baskets that could be used to float babies and valuables when fording rivers. Both face and body painting were common on ceremonial occasions.

The Monos lived in villages of up to about eight houses arranged in a semicircle, and cooperated with nearby villages for marriage exchanges, hunts, funerals, and other social events. The Western and Eastern Mono when combined probably numbered 4,000 before 1770, reduced to 1,500 by 1910.

The Monos are now part of the mixed tribal group of the Tule River Reservation and have almost completely merged with Yokuts at Tule River and in Tulare, Fresno, and Madera counties. They also live at North Fork, Big Sandy, and Cold Springs, where about 1,000 descendants are still reported separately.

## CENSUS 2000

The numbers recorded for the Monocan peoples were:

| | |
|---|---|
| Monocan Indian Nation | 707 |
| Mono | 1,643 |
| North Fork Rancheria | 41 |
| Cold Springs Rancheria | 43 |
| Big Sandy Rancheria | 17 |
| Total | 2,451 |

Below: Western Mono (Monache) bark house, c. 1860. The Monaches used conical thatched, oval earth, and conical bark houses, sharing the first two forms with the Yokuts, Eastern Monos, and Northern Paiutes; the third was primarily Monache, as suitable bark was only available at their higher elevations on the western slopes of the Sierra Nevada. The bark house was unexcavated, with a center post (or two with a ridge beam) supporting a few large poles covered with cedar bark slabs.

# NEZ PERCE

Above: **Nez Perce woman at a recent powwow.**

The most important tribe of the Sahaptian branch of the Penutian language family occupied lands between the Bitterroot Mountains in the east and the junction of the Snake and Columbia rivers in the west. They made their homes along the Clearwater and Snake rivers and in the Wallowa Valley in what is now Idaho, southeastern Washington, and northeastern Oregon. *Nez Percé* is French for "pierced nose," although in fact, unlike many of the other peoples encountered by traders in the nineteenth century, the Nez Perces did not really pierce their noses. They called themselves Tsoop-Nit-Pa-Loo, which means "the Walking Out People," or Nimi'ipuu, which means the "real people" or "we the people."

The Nez Perces first obtained horses early in the eighteenth century, and this quickly transformed them from a traveling hunter-gatherer people to the culture and society of Plains Indian–style buffalo hunters. They were soon masters of horse breeding and riding and became militarily the most powerful of the Plateau tribes. Raiding and war played a major part in Nez Perce ideals of masculine achievement, and they fought frequent battles with all nearby peoples. At times they allied with other Plateau tribes (including the Flathead, Coeur d'Alene, and Spokan) to defend against Plains groups such as the Crow and Blackfeet. Another occasional alliance was with the Cayuse, Umatilla, Yakima, and Walla Walla against the Shoshone and Bannock. Weapons used by the Nez Perce were cedar or ash bows firing obsidian- or jasper-tipped arrows (these were sometimes poisoned with rattlesnake venom), together with spears. Prisoners taken on these raids could be kept as slaves, although many were eventually incorporated into the tribe, and any children they had became free.

Chiefs, who were usually elected, led village and tribal councils that reached decisions by agreement. Each small local band led by a chief had one or more

Below: **Nez Perce men and women, c. 1907. Note the upright eagle feather headdress worn by the man kneeling, and the fine beaded shirt and leggings worn by the young man on the right.**

villages and its own accepted fishing grounds and root crop gathering sites. The Nez Perces moved with the seasons along old established routes within their territories to take best advantage of whatever food was available at each time of the year. Important plant foods included camas, cous (or cowish), wild carrot, and berries. Salmon was the most significant fish caught, but trout, eel, and sturgeon were also taken. In later years, buffalo hunted on the Plains replaced elk, moose, and mountain sheep as the main quarry of Nez Perce hunters.

Traditionally, they wore untailored skins and cedar bark clothing, but by the nineteenth century they began to sew skin garments of typical Plains style instead, although some of the women retained their distinctive fez-shaped basketry hats. Both men and women used a large range of tools locally made from bone, stone, and wood, as well as knives obtained through trade. Women made fine baskets with a range of uses for food collection, preparation, and storage. Other arts included pictorial images on rocks, blankets, and tipi coverings, and embroidery with porcupine quills.

They traded widely, obtaining items such as abalone and dentalium shells from the Pacific coast as well as buffalo products on the Plains. The Nez Perces made huge tipi-style communal houses, up to 150 feet (46 m) in length, by covering wood frames with cedar bark, plaited mats, grasses, and earth. Up to fifty families could sleep along the walls and keep warm around a row of fires down the center. In other areas, smaller winter dwellings were made in the form of circular houses dug into the ground for insulation and roofed over. In summer, temporary brush shelters were sufficient. In the 1800s, many Nez Perces adopted Plains-type tipis.

Through rituals that included fasting and spiritual purification, the Nez Perce believed they could identify and communicate with spirits that would give them strength and

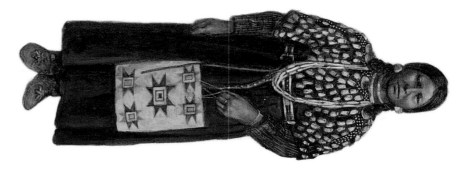

Above: **Nez Perce woman, c. 1900.** Cloth replaced hide late in the nineteenth century. The dress's square-cut yoke gave a "bat wing" effect, with sleeves finished above the elbow; it was worn over a blouse. The yoke was often decorated with cowrie shells, and elk's teeth or carved bone imitations; the main source for this example seems to show brass studs, an unusual addition. Nez Perce moccasins were usually made with side seams. Floral beaded designs appeared quite early during the fur trade era in the Plateau region.

protection. In the course of winter ceremonies, people dressed as their guardian spirits and sang their songs. Shamans, both men and women, who felt access to particularly powerful spirits, acted as religious leaders, weather specialists, and healers.

The Nez Perce had their first direct contact with non-Natives in 1805, when the explorers Lewis and Clark passed through their territory. The travelers remained with the Nez Perce for some time, waiting for snow in the high mountain passes ahead to melt, and left their horses in their care until the return journey. Despite their warlike culture, they welcomed these powerful strangers, and the numerous white missionaries and traders who followed them in the next decades. Although these friendly relations allowed some Nez Perce to gain from the fur trade, new exposure to epidemics of unintentionally imported European diseases wiped out a high proportion of the Indian population.

Between 1855 and 1877, the Nez Perces received a number of allocations of reservation land, each of which was cut back and disregarded by the authorities, settlers, and gold miners. A treaty signed without tribal authority by a single Nez Perce chief in 1863 provided the federal government with a pretext for larger evictions and finally ended friendly relations with the whites. An important leader in the conflict that followed was Chief Looking Glass, who had gained tactical experience fighting on the Plains as an ally of the Crow against the Sioux in 1874.

One of the most famous events in Nez Perce history began with an eviction order in 1877 that gave the Wallowa Band thirty days to quit their lands. Eighty-three Nez Perces, including fifty women and children, were killed when the U.S. Army made a dawn attack on a sleeping camp. Some responded by attacking a group of whites. Joseph, the Wallowa chief, reluctantly backed them, and when soldiers broke a truce to fire on an Indian delegation, he led the men in returning fire. Chief Joseph refused to submit to the inevitable revenge and punishment, instead deciding with other elders to lead the band to Canada. Over the following

Left: Nez Perce beaded heavy leather saddle bag or pommel bag, c. 1900.

two months some 450 Indians made an epic journey of 1,700 miles, evading capture by thousands of U.S. Army troops. Tragically, many died of exhaustion and hunger along the way, and the survivors were finally forced to surrender to Generals Nelson Miles and Oliver Howard just forty miles short of safety across the Canadian border. Only a very few, led by White Bird, did succeed in crossing into Canada, although, perhaps inevitably, they found only further hardship there.

Chief Joseph and his people were sent to Fort Leavenworth in Kansas as prisoners of war following Joseph's surrender at the Bear Paw Battle. Despite public protests over the years that followed, they were kept in poor conditions in camps, with many more falling victim to disease. By 1885, when the War Department finally acted on an Indian Bureau proposal to return them to the reservations, only 282 were still alive out of the 431 who had been taken prisoner. Chief Joseph himself was sent to the Colville Reservation in northern Washington rather than being allowed to return to his home territory. He continued to campaign for the restoration of the lands and rights of his people until his death in September 1904. Despite its tragic conclusion, the heroic flight of Chief Joseph and his followers (in fact they had several leaders, but Joseph is the best remembered today) has become a defining event in the history of the Nez Perce and a key to their sense of identity in the present. His surrender speech is regarded as a testament to human dignity in adversity.

Many of the remaining Nez Perce succumbed to tuberculosis in the final decades of the nineteenth century. Numbers fell from perhaps 6,000 in the early nineteenth century; in 1895, 1,457 were on the reservation at Lapwai, in Idaho; in 1906, 1,534, and 83 on the Colville Reservation. Contemporary Nez Perces are divided between two reservations. At the Nez Perce Reservation in Clearwater, Idaho, there

## I WILL FIGHT NO MORE FOREVER

Surrender Speech by Chief Joseph of the Nez Perce

"I am tired of fighting. Our chiefs are killed. Looking Glass is dead. Toohulhulsote is dead. The old men are all dead. It is the young men who say yes or no. He who led the young men is dead.

"It is cold and we have no blankets. The little children are freezing to death. My people, some of them, have run away to the hills and have no blankets, no food. No one knows where they are—perhaps freezing to death. I want to have time to look for my children and see how many I can find. Maybe I shall find them among the dead.

"Hear me, my chiefs. I am tired. My heart is sick and sad. From where the sun now stands, I will fight no more forever."

Below: Corn husk bag, Nez Perce, c. 1880. The Nez Perce are famed for their large twined storage bags of cornhusk with designs in native fibers or traded wool; the designs probably influenced the rather massive quality of late Plateau beadwork.

were some 1,860 residents in 1990 on 92,685 acres (37,510 ha) of land, while at Colville in Washington State the 1990 population was 3,782 on over a million acres (404,700 ha). Census 2000 reported 3,983 Nez Perce and 2,552 more with part ancestry.

They now earn income from farming, logging, land leases, and tourism. Although very few young people are able to speak the Nez Perce language, the tribal council is heading efforts to preserve it by publishing a dictionary and other texts. The Indian Shaker church, the Native American Church, and the Seven Drum religion, followed by some members of the Chief Joseph Band of Nez Perce, contribute to aspects of continuing cultural vitality, as do annual festivals and traditional dances.

## CORNHUSK AND BEAD BAGS OF THE NEZ PERCE

The Nez Perce, like neighboring peoples, had a long tradition of making small bags from twined grass or thin roots. The small bags were used to carry and store food and were often given as gifts full of cooked food roots or meat to hosts when visiting. Once confined to the reservations from the mid-nineteenth century, people could no longer forage for the most suitable materials as before, and they began to make bags from corn husks, wool, and cotton twine instead. Designs on these bags (which usually were different on each side) included arrows, stars, crosses, and sometimes other more complex traditional symbols, mixing colored wools with dyed corn husks.

From about 1830, as trading contacts with incoming whites increased, glass beaded bags began to be made, both for local use and later for sale to whites. Italian glass beads, called "pony beads," were used in the early examples, with smaller Italian-made "seed" beads more common after 1860. The bags were made from either leather or trade cloth, sewn with sinew or cotton thread. Using an iron needle (bought from a trader) on a cloth bag allowed finer detailing than was possible when working with an awl on thicker leather. Geometrical designs similar to those on corn husk bags soon gave way to increasingly complex pictorial patterns of flowers and animals. Like basket making, beadwork embroidery became one of the major means of artistic expression for women of the Nez Perce and other Plateau peoples.

## SOUTHERN PAIUTE

The term now used to cover around sixteen small bands of people in southern Utah and Nevada, including parts of Arizona above the Colorado River and extended to include the Chemehuevi of San Bernardino County, California, who spoke related variations of the Numic-Shoshonean branch of the Uto-Aztecan language family. A speaker of one Southern Paiute language would be able to understand the others, but not the languages spoken by the nearby Northern Paiute. They can be divided for convenience into a number of subgroups—Moapa, Shivwits, Pahranagat, Kaibab, Kaiparowits, Panaca, and so on, but there was no tribal organization. Instead, they divided into much smaller family-based bands (usually ten to fifteen households) that held together for mutual aid and subsistence collaboration. The name *Paiute* is thought to mean "true Ute" or "water Ute," and some sources argue that it was applied to the Northern Paiute only after 1850. They called themselves *Nuwu*, which meant "person."

The Southern Paiute, like other Great Basin people, obtained most of their food through hunting and gathering. This daily quest for food kept them on the move throughout their territory in routes dictated by the seasons of the year, as they visited the best places to search for small game, grasshoppers, gophers, fish, nuts, seeds, and wild vegetables. Men used huge nets in communal hunts for rabbits and other small game. They hunted larger game using bows made from cedar wood. If a boy who had not reached puberty killed an animal, the meat was given away to the elders of the family. Women gathered wild plants such as roots, grass seeds, nuts, juniper berries, and agave. Seeds were ground and made into either a mush or a kind of bread. There was some very limited agriculture, with corn, beans, and squash grown in small plots on floodplains.

In the winter, some Southern Paiute lived in caves, while others made gabled or conical houses of willow and earth or cedar brush on a pole frame. In the summer, more simple brush shelters were used, and by

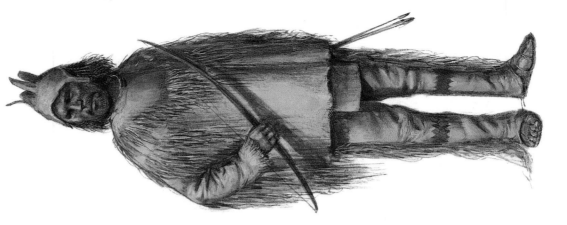

Below: **Southern Paiute man, c. 1872. At this date John Wesley Powell (later of the Smithsonian Institution) and photographer John K. Hillers recorded Southern Paiute men and women wearing buckskin clothing which resembled that of the Ute and Shoshone. It is unconfirmed that this clothing is Paiute; however, the buckskin cap and sandals are more typically Paiute.**

## COYOTE AND MONSTER: A PLATEAU LEGEND

Coyote tales, in numerous versions, are told throughout the Plateau and beyond.

Coyote is a wise and mischievous figure who established the landscape and laws of the Plateau. Here Coyote kills an Elk monster east of the Bitterroot Valley (in Montana). Coyote tells Mole, his wife, to dig a tunnel so he can reach the Elk monster. The monster is taken by surprise and scared by Coyote's power to reach him unnoticed.

Coyote tricks the monster into following him down the tunnel. In the dark it falls into a hole dug by Mole. Coyote calls loudly, as if he were calling to an enemy ahead of them. The monster climbs out of the hole, tries to run, but falls into one hole after another. At last Coyote says, "Let me carry your shield, then you can run faster." Coyote puts the shield on his back, but the monster still falls into another hole Mole had dug. "Let me carry your spear," Coyote says. Soon he gets the monster's knife and all of his equipment. Then Coyote runs around, shouting, "This is how we charge the enemy." And he jabs the monster with the spear. He does this four times, each time yelling that he had taken something from the enemy. The fifth time he jabs the monster, he yells, "I have stripped the enemy." Then he says to the Elk monster, "You can never kill anyone again."

the middle of the nineteenth century some had started to use Plains-style skin tipis copied from the Ute. Robes made from rabbit fur were worn during cold weather, but in the summer both men and women wore only small skin aprons or loincloths. Skin caps were worn by men, basketry caps by women, and sandals were made from bark or yucca fibers.

Southern Paiute women made fine decorated basketry, and other art in the region included small wood carvings and some rock art. They were a generally peaceful people who suffered slave raiding from more aggressive neighbors such as the Ute, Navajo, and the Spanish in New Mexico. An exception was the Chemehuevi group, who at the end of the eighteenth century wiped out bands of desert Mohave and took over their land.

The Southern Paiutes may have encountered the Spanish from the sixteenth century, but they didn't feel much impact from Euro-American contact until early in the nineteenth century, when they were driven from much of their best land by slave-raiding Spanish ranchers and American fur trappers. Mormon settlers, who arrived in significant numbers after 1850, took the best of the remaining land for settlements and soon reduced many Paiutes to starvation and begging. The Pyramid Lake War in 1860, begun because white traders kidnapped and raped two Southern Paiute girls, finally defeated the tribe. Although the U. S. government tried to confine them to the Uintah Reservation, most fled to deserted areas of southern Utah. By the 1870s, starvation and disease had reduced the Southern Paiute population by as much as 80 percent. The survivors found what work they could in towns, or were gradually settled on reservations.

Their present descendants have been connected with the following reservations: Moapa River on the Muddy River, southern Nevada (150); Shivwits, Kanosh, Koosharem, Indian Peaks, and Kanarraville, all terminated in 1930, which again caused great hardship and exploitation. In 1970, the U.S. government settled a $7.25 million lawsuit with the Southern Paiutes, admitting they had wrongfully taken Paiute land. They were not finally restored as the "Paiute Indian

Tribe of Utah" until 1980 (200); Kaibab in northern Arizona (150); Las Vegas Colony, Nevada (100); Chemehuevi Valley Reservation, Arizona (500); and Colorado River Reservation, Arizona (350). Only about half live on their reservations, and there are long-standing off-reservation communities. In 1992, there were 1,556 Southern Paiutes, exclusive of the Chemehuevi, who numbered c. 900.

Today, the federal government recognizes five Southern Paiute bands as tribal entities. These are the Kaibab Band of Paiute Indians, the Las Vegas Tribe of Paiute Indians, the Moapa Band of Paiute Indians, the Paiute Indian Tribe of Utah, and the San Juan Paiute Tribe. Of these, the Las Vegas Colony is the most successful economically, with low living standards and high rates of unemployment typical elsewhere. For Census 2000 figures see boxes on pages 34 and 39.

## NORTHERN PAIUTE

A term that covers Numic-speaking bands of the Uto-Aztecan language family which, together with the Mono of California, make up the Western Numic branch. Northern Paiutes called themselves *Numa*, which means simply "People," and were sometimes known to white settlers as Digger Indians (a derogatory term), Snakes, and Paviotso. The Bannock Indians are also of Northern Paiute origin. "Northern Paiute" is a relatively recent, general term: There were important cultural differences among different bands, and although they had a shared language, they had no overall political unity. The Northern Paiutes lived in a vast area from Mono Lake in California, in the south, through the Walker and Humboldt River drainages, into northwest Nevada, north beyond Malheur Lake, Oregon, and west into northeast California. Much of their land was scrub desert and freshwater marshes. They also ranged around lakes, mountains, rivers, and on the high plains.

Like other Great Basin peoples, the Northern Paiute were seminomadic gatherers who relied on whatever seeds, berries, and roots the women could collect, together with some hunting and

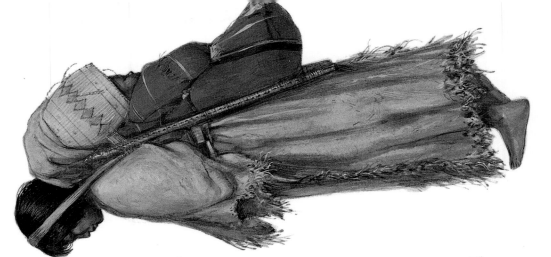

Below: Paiute, c. 1880. The cradle has a flat, wedge-shaped foundation of willow rods with an inverted U-shaped top, covered with buckskin or canvas. A basketry awning protects and shelters the child's head.

**Right: Southern Paiute baskets, c. 1880. Woman with twined conical burden basket on chest tumpline, and close-coiled tray used to sift mesquite meal.**

## CENSUS 2000

The numbers recorded for the Paiute were:

| | |
|---|---|
| Bridgeport Paiute Indian Colony | 3 |
| Burns Paiute tribe | 155 |
| Cedarville Rancheria | 7 |
| Fort Bidwell | 45 |
| Fort Independence | 4 |
| Kaibab Band of Paiute Indians | 153 |
| Las Vegas Tribe of the Las Vegas Indian Colony | 49 |
| Lovelock Paiute Tribe of the Lovelock Indian Colony | 125 |
| Moapa Band of Paiute | 103 |
| Northern Paiute | 223 |
| Paiute | 5,900 |
| Pyramid Lake | 1,274 |
| San Juan Southern Paiute | 10 |
| Southern Paiute | 127 |
| Summit Lake | 31 |
| Susanville | 49 |
| Utu Utu Gwaitu Paiute | 42 |
| Walker River | 931 |
| Winnemucca | 3 |
| Yerington Paiute | 427 |
| Yahooskin Band of Snake | 10 |
| **Total** | **9,705** |
| Chemehuevi | 696 |

fishing. They dug up roots with fire-hardened sticks, and ate them raw or dried them in the sun. Pine nuts and acorns were ground up and boiled to make gruel. They drove rabbits and other small rodents, important sources of meat, into huge nets on communal hunts. The men also hunted birds, squirrels, and bigger game such as elk and buffalo. When a boy made his first large kill there was a coming-of-age ceremony in which the youth stood on a pile of sagebrush to chew the meat with sage, then placed it on his joints to give himself strength. In some areas fish, especially salmon, were also an important resource. Some bands also cultivated wild plants on a small scale.

Northern Paiute dwellings varied throughout the region and changed with the seasons. In the summer, many lived in wickiups, small huts of reed brush spread over willow pole frames. In the north, winter houses had frameworks spread with mats and covered with a layer of earth to keep in the warmth from the fire, while in the mountains winter houses were dug into the ground and roofed over. When people died they were wrapped in their skin blankets and buried along with their possessions. Their families mourned for a year, cutting off their hair and covering their faces with ashes. The Northern Paiutes had both male and female shaman healers and religious leaders. They cured by giving herbal potions, sucking out sickness, and, for some diseases, by rituals designed to restore a straying soul to the patient's body. The Northern Paiutes, particularly the Bannock, were more warlike than the Southern Paiutes, fighting with bow and arrow, spears, and clubs, against enemies such as the Blackfeet and Crow.

The Northern Paiutes and Shoshones tried to stop the tide of white miners and traders from taking over their lands during the mid-1800s, most intensely in the Snake War of 1866–67, which ended with the federal government's promise to protect the Paiutes from white harassment, a promise they failed to keep. Important to the painful transition to reservation life was Winnemucca, who led a band of several hundred Northern Paiutes in demanding a

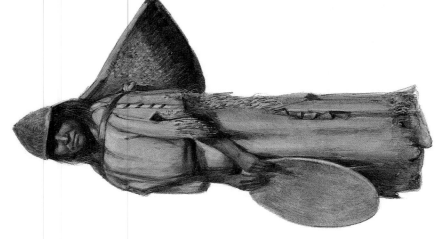

reservation of their own. His daughter Sarah Winnemucca established a school at Lovelock, Nevada, and in 1884 published *Life Among the Paiutes*. In 1889, a Northern Paiute called Wovoka, known to whites as Jack Wilson, developed a new, important Ghost Dance movement (see box, below).

Despite short-lived resistance, many Northern Paiutes were ultimately placed on reservations, with total populations given as 3,038 in 1910; 4,420 Northern and Southern Paiute in 1930; 2,590 in 1950; and 5,123 in 1980. The largest reservation populations are at Pyramid Lake, Walker River, and Fort McDermitt in Nevada, but others are at Benton and Bridgeport, Mono County, California; Burns, Warm Springs, and Klamath Lake, Oregon (mixed with other tribes); Duck Valley, Nevada (with Shoshone); Summit Lake, Winnemucca, Lovelock, Fallon, Reno-Sparks, and Yerington, Nevada; Fort Bidwell, XL Ranch, Cedarville, and Alturas in Modoc County, California (mixed with Pit River); and Susanville, Lassen County, California (mixed with Maidu). See box at left for Census 2000 figures.

## WOVOKA AND THE PAIUTE GHOST DANCE

Wovoka, a Paiute who was born in Nevada in the mid-1850s and grew up a Christian with the name Jack Wilson, was the key figure in a new religious movement known as the Ghost Dance that spread rapidly among many Indian tribes east of the Missouri River in 1889–90. In 1889, he had a vision in which an Indian messiah promised that the old Indian lifestyle would return through a revitalized earth rich with buffalo and game that would spread from the West, pushing the whites back to their own land and reuniting the surviving Indians in immortality with the thousands who had died from disease and hunger. In the meantime, they should abandon all violence and live in honesty and peace. The central ritual of the Ghost Dance was a circular dance in which men and women held hands and sang the ghost songs, without musical accompaniment, while the priests in the center of the circle induced visions of the future paradise. Despite Wovoka's peaceful message, the revival of Indian values was viewed as a threat by whites and the U.S. government.

Among the warlike Sioux it took a more aggressive form, with Ghost Dance shirts promising the wearer immunity from bullets, and sporadic unrest culminating in the death of Sitting Bull and the massacre at Wounded Knee, South Dakota. The fervor of the movement gradually faded after several dates for the promised return passed uneventfully. Wovoka survived the collapse of the Ghost Dance, living on as Jack Wilson until 1932.

Below: Kneeling Shoshone woman, c. 1890. Pine board covered with buckskin, the area above the bag is elaborately beaded in geometric or floralistic designs—probably quite a late development. The laced bag front had minor variations for gender, allowing for the insertion of a soft diaper pad between the legs of infant girls, or with holes in the central flap tied over the lacing which allowed infant boys to urinate outside the buckskin pouch.

# EASTERN or WIND RIVER SHOSHONE

The ancestors of the Eastern and Northern Shoshone are probably the "Snakes" or "Gens du Serpent" reported by the earliest white traders. Ranging as far north as the Saskatchewan River, they were later expelled from the western Plains by the Blackfeet, who were armed with newly obtained guns. Ultimately they were restricted to areas of the Plateau and Basin—except for the Eastern Shoshones, who have occupied western Wyoming periodically since about A.D. 1500, particularly in the watersheds of the Snake, Wind, and Sweetwater Rivers. The Comanche split from them in the eighteenth century and moved south into Texas. The Eastern Shoshones formed two groups, the Mountain Sheep Eaters in the north, and the Buffalo Eaters in the south and east. Culturally, they were intermediate between Plains, Basin, and Plateau—gatherers of berries and roots, but also experienced buffalo hunters whose women were noted as skilled and rapid butchers. Dried buffalo and smoked fish dominated the winter diet.

The Eastern Shoshones had lived on the Great Plains since around 1500, and acquired horses around 1700. As a result, their material goods and way of life closely resembled that of the true Plains people; their tipis, ritual objects, horse equipment, and ceremonialism, including the Sun Dance, reflected their association with Plains culture. The Sun Dance was a three-day and four-night-long ceremony centered on ten poles erected around a mounted buffalo head, in which male dancers demonstrated their strength and access to supernatural spirit powers. The Sun Dance, as well as the other two important community rituals, known as the Father and the Shuffling (Ghost) Dances, were intended to promote the welfare of the group and of the natural resources on which they depended. Chiefs, who lived in distinctive painted tipis, had authority over hunting, migration, and defense. The Eastern Shoshones separated into three to five

Above: **Shoshone man.**

bands during the winter before reuniting each spring and summer for the buffalo hunt and Sun Dance.

They remained generally on good terms with whites during the nineteenth century through the efforts of Chief Washakie, and grew quite wealthy from fur trading with the settlers. As a result, they were initially granted a huge reservation of 44 million acres (17.8 million ha), in a treaty of 1868, but within a few years this was cut to less than 2 million (.80 million ha). There was great resentment when, in 1878, the Arapaho, whom the Shoshone had fought against in alliance with the U.S. Army, were placed on the same reservation. Their traditional economy, based on the buffalo, ended with the virtual extinction of the great herds, leaving the Eastern Shoshones to endure great hardship on their reservation. By the early twentieth century, average life expectancy had fallen to little over twenty years. A gradual process of improvement began in the 1930s and gained momentum in the 1960s. Today a modified Sun Dance with some Christian elements is shared with the Northern Shoshone, Ute, and Crow, and has been an important element in reservation life. The Peyote religion and Pan-Indianism, including annual powwows, are also a continuing part of Shoshone life. For Census 2000 figures, see the box on page 39.

## NORTHERN SHOSHONE

The Northern Shoshone were bands of Numic-speaking Shoshoneans living in the Snake River Valley, Idaho, and as far north as the Salmon River. Linguistically very close to the Western Shoshones, their environment was marginally Plateau, where it merges into the Great Basin. They depended on salmon and other fish, collecting wild roots such as yampa, bitterroot, and camas, and hunting game such as antelope, deer, mountain sheep, and bison. Groups were named after their main foods, including "Salmon-Eaters" and "Mountain Sheep-Eaters" around the Salmon and Lemhi rivers, and "Yampa-Eaters" of the Camas Prairie. Some bands of mixed Shoshone and Paiute lived on the Oregon border.

Opposite: **Roadside sign advertising Shoshone radio station.**

Above: **Shoshone man.**

Historical evidence suggests the Shoshones may have been the "Snakes" who occupied the northern Plains before the Blackfeet pushed them west of the Rockies; nevertheless, they took on elements of Plains culture, hunting bison in the Montana plains in the nineteenth century. They developed trade relations with the Crow and also adopted the Plains-style Grass Dance and the Sun Dance, to which they added Christian features; their form of Sun Dance is now shared with the Crow and Wind River Shoshone.

Most Northern Shoshones lived in conical homes made from grass, sagebrush, or willow branches, but the Fort Hall and Lemhi groups adopted Plains-style tipis. For their most elaborate art form they painted or beaded geometric designs on rawhide. Annual trading fairs were held where goods such as dried salmon and skins were traded for horses and mules, with trading partners such as the Nez Perce, Crow, and Flathead.

Mythological beings such as Wolf and Coyote played an important role in Northern Shoshone legends of creation and tribal origins, but religious life for individuals centered around spirits found in the course of dreams and visions. These spirits would advise people as to what medicines they should take, what foods should be avoided, and other means to achieve success. Most people traveled in temporary bands, some of which had chiefs with limited authority. The power of Chiefs did increase among groups who moved onto the Plains, where activities such as buffalo hunting required a higher level of organization and leadership.

The Shoshones had obtained horses by the late seventeenth century, which they then used to become travelers and traders. Whites established trading posts within Bannock and Shoshone territory as early as 1810, and the Shoshones participated in the annual summer rendezvous with white fur trappers on the Green River in Wyoming. Independent life ended in the 1860s when the Lemhi and Fort Hall reservations were founded, although Lemhi was closed in 1907 and the population moved to Fort Hall. There are no reliable population figures for Shoshone before white contact, although it has been estimated that there were perhaps over 15,000 before epidemics of imported diseases took their heavy toll. An estimate for 1860 gives 3,000 Shoshone and Bannock; in 1937, 3,650 "Northern Shoshone" were reported, and in 1983, about 3,900 were enrolled at Fort Hall Reservation, Idaho. The Shoshones and Bannocks still hold annual festivals, powwows, and rodeos, including their Sun Dance at Fort Hall, despite overwhelming modern influences.

## WESTERN SHOSHONE

A collective name for a group of scattered bands extending from the arid Death Valley of California through the highlands of central Nevada into northwestern Utah, including the upper reaches of the Owyhee and Humboldt Rivers. They belonged to the Numic division of the Shoshonean or Uto-Aztecan language family, with most Western Shoshones speaking Panamint, Shoshone, or Comanche. Usually designated in small subgroups such as the "Pine Nut Eaters," two groups are sometimes given separate status: the Panamints on the west side of Death Valley, Inyo County, California, and the Gosiutes of western Utah (also known as Goshutes, they are ethnic Shoshone but are now regarded as legally distinct following a 1962 court ruling). The group called the Weber Utes of

### CENSUS 2000

The numbers recorded for the Shoshone were:

| | |
|---|---|
| Duckwater | 139 |
| Ely | 100 |
| Goshute | 222 |
| Shoshone | 6,672 |
| Skull Valley Band of Goshute Indians | 14 |
| Death Valley Band of Goshute Indians | 201 |
| Northwestern Band of Shoshoni Nation of Utah (Washakie) | 132 |
| Wind River (Eastern Shoshone) | 110 |
| Yomba | 102 |
| Total | 7,739 |

**Te-Moak Tribes of Western Shoshone Indians of Nevada**

| | |
|---|---|
| Te-Moak Tribes | 926 |
| Battle Mountain | 5 |
| Elko | 15 |
| Wells Band | 3 |
| Total | 949 |

**Paiute-Shoshone**

| | |
|---|---|
| Duck Valley | 120 |
| Fallon | 532 |
| Fort McDermitt Paiute and Shoshone Tribes | 306 |
| Shoshone Paiute | 1,943 |
| Bishop | 157 |
| Lone Pine | 10 |
| Big Pine Band of Owens Valley Paiute-Shoshone | 33 |
| Total | 3,112 |

| | |
|---|---|
| Shoshone-Bannock Tribes of the Fort Hall Reservation | 4,587 |

Above: **Early twentieth century photograph of Soshone youths.**

the Great Salt Lake are also classified as Western Shoshone.

Shoshone culture was of the Great Basin type: They relied on plant gathering for subsistence, together with harvesting nuts and seeds and some hunting. They threshed, roasted, and ground seeds, then boiled them into a kind of gruel or thin porridge. Face and body painting was common, and both sexes wore only limited clothing, mostly skin garments, despite the harsh climate. The Shoshone produced very fine coiled basketry which was important in collecting and winnowing seeds, while they used waterproof baskets to transport drinking water from distant springs and lakes. Western Shoshones played games, including shinny, ball racing, hoop and pole, jacks, dice, and four sticks. Most groups had shamans who healed the sick by techniques including the laying on of hands. A major deity was the sun, called Apo. They had chiefs or group headmen but these held only very limited powers. The Western Shoshones traded salt and rabbit skins to groups such as the Paiutes for shell money and buckskins.

White settlers, miners, and ranchers followed the earlier explorations of Jedediah Smith and John C.

Frémont. Mormons began arriving on Gosiute lands in 1847, and the discovery of gold in 1857 brought a huge influx of settlers. In 1863 a treaty with the United States established reservations, notably Duck Valley on the Nevada-Idaho border, but not until after 1900 did any substantial numbers of Western Shoshones occupy the "colonies" scattered in their old territory. The number living on reservations peaked at 50 percent in 1927.

Most Western Shoshones slipped unnoticed into the white people's mode of living, but at a low economic level, as seasonal workers on ranches or in mines. Their population may have been over 3,000 before white contact; in 1937, 1,201 were reported, including Gosiute and Panamint; and in 1980, 2,923. For Census 2000 figures, see the box on page 29.

Hand games and fandangos (fast dances) are still frequently held, and most surviving groups are making efforts to preserve their language.

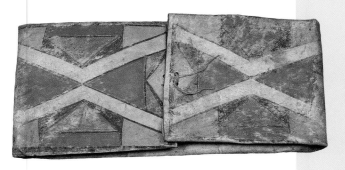

Below: **Parfleche decorated with geometric shapes.**

## ART OF THE SHOSHONE

Among the important arts of the Shoshone were beadwork, hide painting, and parfleche (rawhide) containers. The Shoshone also displayed creativity in other aspects of their material culture such as basketry and children's toys.

In their early (pre-1890) beadwork the Shoshone used mainly white, green, blue, and cobalt beads, with some yellow, primarily to make panels of geometric designs on clothing and pouches. After that, their geometric designs gradually gave way to floral motifs, which over the decades of the twentieth century became increasingly realistic. After the

1950s, their dominant design became the vivid red "Shoshone Rose." They used beadwork to decorate a huge range of items made both for sale and for use in powwows and other cultural events.

Shoshone hide painters used homemade mineral paints to decorate hides used for tipis, buffalo skin robes, and other garments. In the early years on the reservations they were also made for sale. Their paintings depicted buffalo hunts, battles, and episodes from the stories of famous individuals and bands. Chief Washakie (c. 1804–1900) is remembered as a great hide painter.

Parfleche are containers made from rawhide which were painted with mostly geometric designs, usually made and decorated by women. Shoshone baskets, which they usually made from willow, were more functional than elaborately decorated, and they sold few to outsiders. Basket making, unlike beadwork, has virtually died out among the Shoshone. Today the Wind River Historical Center in Wyoming documents the history of Shoshone art, tracing the development of beadwork and other expressions from the few surviving pieces from the early 1800s to the continuing traditions of today.

Below: Ute man, c. 1885. Men's shirts had long triangular neck flaps, probably an exaggeration of the original hide shape (or representing knife sheaths worn from the neck by eastern tribes). Their shirts and leggings were usually heavily fringed, with beaded strips in large triangular and stair-stepped designs.

The Ute are a Shoshonean (Uto-Aztecan) people of central western Colorado, central eastern Utah, and the far northern part of New Mexico, occupying the drainages and tributaries of the Green and Colorado rivers to the west of the Rocky Mountains. The name "Ute" is thought to be of Spanish origin, but they called themselves Nunt'z, which means "the people." They are closely connected to the Southern Paiute in language, together forming the southern Numic branch of the Uto-Aztecan language family.

Their historic culture reflected both Great Basin and Plains traits; eastern and southern bands hunted bison, but they also collected berries, roots, nuts, and seeds. They were divided into a number of subtribes: Capote and Moache in southern Colorado; Wiminuche north of the San Juan River; Uncompahgre in the area of the Gunnison River, Colorado; White River Ute, including the Yampa, on the White, Yampa, and Green rivers; Uintah in northeastern Utah; Pahvant around Sevier Lake; Timpanogot around Utah Lake; Sanpit around Manti in the Sanpete Valley; and Moanunt or Fish Ute on the upper course of the Sevier River, Utah. In later years they were concentrated in four bands—Uncompahgre, White River, Uintah, and Wiminuche. They were known to the Spanish from the 1600s, and they raided the Hopi, Paiute, and Plains tribes. However, from 1750 onward Apache, Arapaho, and Cheyenne exploited Ute hunting grounds in their eastern mountain valleys.

Although descended from the so-called Fremont people (c. A.D. 900), early agriculturists who were possibly a subdivision of the Anasazi farther south, the Utes were hunters and gatherers like other Great Basin and Plateau peoples. Their major plant foods were seeds and berries, pine nuts, and yucca. Buffalo were their most significant game, but they also hunted deer,

*Above: Ute warrior wearing shirt and leggings typically decorated with broad beadwork strips and, essential to the Bear Dance, many bells; note characteristic beaded strips of the leggings around his ankles, and the broad bandolier strap over his left shoulder.*

beaver, elk, fowl, and sage hens. Some groups used insects (such as locusts) as an important protein source, while others fished for trout and chub.

Eastern Utes lived in buffalo hide tipis, while farther west, domed houses were made out of woven willow branches. Cone-shaped pole-frame shelters covered with juniper bark mats were also used. As with other Great Basin groups who adopted the horse for buffalo hunting, the older system of family groups led by elders gradually gave way to more formal expressions of leadership, as band chiefs became necessary to organize the larger numbers needed for successful hunting. In fact, the Utes became one of the earliest Indian peoples to begin the adaptation to a mounted life, after they began to use horses—received from the Spanish in exchange for buckskins and Indian captive and slaves, among other valuables, in the mid and late seventeenth century. In the eighteenth and early nineteenth centuries, mounted bands of the Ute raided the Western Shoshones, Southern Paiutes, and New Mexico Indians.

Among the Utes, both men and women could become shamans who had a role in healing, and in some cases in affecting the weather. All individuals, but especially shamans, tried to access power through personal links to the spirits of animals and plants contacted in dreams and visions. The Utes had both the Sun Dance, derived from their contacts with Plains peoples, and the Bear Dance.

The ten-day-long Bear Dance was held every spring. Led by a specially appointed dance chief and accompanied by a group of men playing musical rasps, the Bear Dance marked the end of girls' coming-of-age ceremonies and was a time for courtship and social renewal after the harsh winter. A Ute myth says that the Bear Dance began after a man dreamed of a bear and followed its instructions to go up into the mountains. There he saw the bear dancing and was taught to do the dance and learned the songs. The musical rasps (notched wooden sticks) used in the Bear Dance are believed to imitate the sounds of the bears waking from their winter hibernation. Many other Indian peoples adopted the Bear Dance from the Ute.

Among the other legends of the Ute is the tale of Sleeping Ute Mountain. According to this story, the land of the region was pushed up into its mountains and valleys long ago, in the course of a battle between the Great Warrior God and the Evil Ones.

Right: The Pauvan or Pahvant were a Ute group in Utah, 1860s.

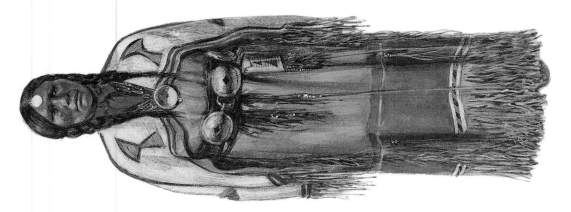

Above: **Ute woman, c. 1885. Late-nineteenth-century costume showed the characteristics of the neighboring Shoshone, Jicarilla Apache, and Plains tribes. Eastern Ute bands adopted lazy stitch beadwork superficially resembling Cheyenne and Arapaho work. Note facial and hair paint; the ankle-length dress is made of two skins (probably deer), tails up, with a fully beaded yoke (sometimes separate) forming the upper part; the silver conch belt is a traded Navajo item.**

The highest mountain is where the wounded Warrior God lay down to sleep, his blood flowing as rivers of vital water. When clouds gather around this high peak, the sign of rain shows that the god is pleased with his people.

Western Utes wore garments of twined sagebrush bark, with beaver or weasel skin caps. Farther east, clothes were made from tanned buckskin, and as contacts with the peoples of the Plains increased, beading, fringes, and other Plains influences spread. The buffalo was also an important source of clothing, as well as contributing to shelter, food, and implements such as bowstrings. The Utes made woven sleeping mats, fine baskets, and, in some districts, coiled pottery.

The first non-native settlement in historic Ute territory was established in Colorado in 1851, and a fort was built the next year to protect it. In the east, hordes of miners came following a gold strike in 1858. Some Utes fought with the incomers against the Navajo, but in the west growing numbers of Mormons had driven them from 90 percent of their land by as early as the 1870s. In 1868, a reservation was established in Colorado for Uncompahgre, Moache, Capote, Wiminuche, Yampa, and Uintah Utes.

It was in this period of turmoil and disaster that Chief Ouray, a band leader of the Tabeguache Southern Ute, emerged as a major figure, becoming recognized (and rewarded) by the U.S. government as the Ute senior chief. He had learned to speak English as a child working on a ranch. A strong advocate of compromise with the whites and of patient negotiation in the face of continued adversity, he is today regarded by many Utes as a key figure in their history. He visited Washington and met with President Rutherford B. Hayes shortly before his death in 1880.

In 1880, following the "Meeker Massacre," two reservations were formed in Utah to become the Uintah and Ouray reservations, and the Uncompahgre and White River Ute were moved there in 1880 and 1882. The Meeker Massacre

Below: Ute family group.

occurred after a government Indian agent attempted to force the White River Utes to give up their traditional lifestyle by methods that included destroying their ponies and instigating an army attack. The agent, Nathan Meeker, was among those killed in the resulting conflict, and the influence of Chief Ouray played a major part in averting a wider war. The Wiminuche, Moache, and Capote were subsequently located on the Southern Ute Agency, along the San Juan River Valley of southern Colorado and adjacent New Mexico—now the Ute Mountain and Southern Ute reservations.

The Utes probably numbered 4,500 before the reservation period, but were reduced to 3,391 by 1885. In 1920 there were 449 Uintah, 257 White River, 421 Uncompahgre (Uintah-Ouray Reservation), and 456 on the Ute Mountain and Southern Ute reservations. In 1980, there were 2,000 Northern Ute, exclusive of 1,000 mixed-ancestory and 900 Southern Ute. Census 2000 reported that there were 7,309 Ute—875 Uintah Ute, 1,478 Ute Mountain, 1,117 Southern Ute, and 3,839 Ute.

Life on the reservations was hard, with poor soils, harsh climates, and lack of capital all impeding the switch to farming that the government was supposedly encouraging. There was terrible suffering in the 1880s when food rations were held back to force Utes on the reservations to send their children to government boarding schools as far away as Albuquerque, New Mexico. Tragically, almost half of the children at these schools died. Prominent Ute leaders in this painful era included Buckskin Charley, who succeeded Ouray as head of the Southern Ute in 1880 until his death in 1936, and Jack House, chief of the Wiminuche from 1936 to 1971.

Real improvements in conditions on the reservations were not seen until the 1950s, when the Confederated Ute Tribes won $31 million in land compensation claims, which was then largely invested in tourist and other enterprises. More money was secured in claims and federal grants over the following decades. Today, economic activities

Above: **Woman with cradle, c. 1895. The Northern Ute probably adopted the Plateau-style cradle late in the nineteenth century, adding an eyeshade of willow basketry. There was some concern over possible harmful effects of confining a baby in a cradle for extended periods, but Native Americans claimed beneficial effects for developing erect posture, apart from ensuring safety during the day. At night a mother would transfer her baby into a soft buckskin bag, or place it in bedding.**

include oil and gas leasing, timber sales, tourism, pottery production, and a gaming operation: The Ute Mountain Casino was opened in 1992, providing several hundred jobs for local people. Despite these activities, however, there is still high unemployment and below-average income on Ute reservations. The Ute language is widely spoken and the Bear Dance and Sun Dance are still prominent festivals. Today, there is also an annual rodeo. The Native American Church is active, while many White Mesa Ute have become Mormons. There are three federal government-recognized tribal entities: the Southern Ute Indian Tribe, the Ute Mountain Tribe, and the Ute Indian Tribe.

## UTE RELIGION

Most Ute religious practice involved a personal and individual focus on obtaining and securing a relationship with spirits through dreams. Unlike most of their neighbors on the Plains, for the Ute the primary purpose of these relationships was to obtain the necessary supernatural powers to act as a shaman or healer, rather than to obtain wealth, success in battle, or other more physical goals. The two main communal ceremonies were the Sun Dance and the Bear Dance. The Sun Dance, which the Ute obtained from Plains Indians, was a major annual festival, involving elaborate dances, costumes, and body painting. As well as being an important social focus bringing together scattered bands, the Sun Dance was a means of raising the power and status of a shaman by establishing his personal bond with the Great Spirit.

The Bear Dance, which originated with the Ute, was held every spring as the snows melted and the winter camps were about to split up. It honors the grizzly bear that taught the Ute to resist the mischievous coyote, and marked the emergence of the bears from their winter hibernation. For three of four days women dance in one line, while the men chosen as their partners dance opposite them in a second line. The Ute called the Bear Dance mama-kwa-nkha-pu, or "woman step dance." The dancing women are the female bears dancing in the spring and express the female principle of reawakened fertility, while the men embody the Ute hunter who first learned the dance from a bear in the forest. Today the Bear Dance is held every June and is a major focus for Ute tribal identity.

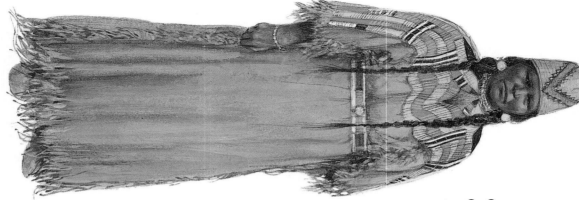

Above: Yakima woman, c. 1885. The older, classic dress of the Plateau and northwestern Plains was constructed of two elk skins forming the front and back, sewn together. To straighten the shoulder line, the tail ends were folded over and stitched down. Plateau women decorated the upper part with bands of large pony beads strung loosely and sewn to the elk skin. Her basket hat of native fiber has a deep triangular design in bear grass embroidery.

This important group of the Sahaptian language family occupied the valley of the Yakima River, a northern tributary of the Columbia on the east side of the Cascade mountain range in present-day Yakima County, Washington. Several small groups are usually given Yakima status: the Kittitas or Upper Yakima, Pshwanwapam, and Mical lived north of the main body; the Taidnapam, who may have been closer to the Klikitat, were in Skamania County; the Topinish, Atanum, Pisko, and others formed minor groups. Lewis and Clark estimated the population of true Yakimas as 1,200 in 1806. Yakima has been translated as "runaway," although other sources suggest it comes from E-yak-ma, meaning "a growing family." The tribe once called themselves Waptailmim, or "people of the Narrow River."

Like many other Plateau tribes, the Yakima acquired horses early in the eighteenth century and began to hunt buffalo on the Great Plains. However, they retained many aspects of their older Plateau lifestyle and culture. Fish, supplemented by roots and berries, remained their major food source. They built winter lodges using a mat- and earth-covered rectangular pole structure which they set into the earth for insulation against the cold. During the winter, a number of families would gather together at a permanent village, while in the summer they spread out to hunt, fish, and search for food.

In 1855, the United States made a treaty with the Yakima and thirteen other smaller tribes and bands by which they ceded their lands, and the Yakima Reservation was established, upon which all the participating bands were to be confederated under the name Yakima and under a distinguished leader, Kamaiakan. However, fighting quickly broke out after gold was discovered and soldiers were sent to protect miners who had attacked Indians. When a Walla Walla chief was murdered, the Walla Walla, Cayuse, Palouse, and Umatilla tribes joined the

Yakimas, at one point attacking the town of Seattle. Unrest continued, with Yakimas leading the 1855 Yakima (or Coeur d'Alene) war as the railroad and white settlers threatened their way of life. Twenty-four Yakima were executed the following year before the tribe agreed to move onto the reservation.

The collective name "Yakima" has for many years been used to designate all the confederate groups on the agency built around the true Yakima, which also includes some Wishram and Wasco of Chinookan origin. This collective group numbered 2,933 in 1937; 6,853 on or adjacent to the reservation in 1984; and 8,315 in 1992. Census 2000 reported 8,481 "Yakama" and 5 "Yakama Cowlitz."

Throughout the 1900s, the tribe lost most of its remaining traditional fishing places due to hydroelectric dam projects. Despite their economic problems, however, much of Yakima culture has been retained, with the language and the Longhouse or Seven Drums religion still thriving. Powwows, rodeos, salmon feasts, and fairs, which today are expressions of Yakima Indian life, are regularly held. There is a large cultural center, museum, and restaurant complex on the reservation, as well as a college, a radio station, and newspapers. The Yakima sacred mountain, Pahto (Mount Adams), was included in 22,000 (9,000 ha) acres of land returned by the government in the 1970s.

## Yakima War of 1855

After the Yakima defeated the U.S. Army in two successive battles, a local militia joined U.S. troops and finally defeated the Yakima and their Native Plateau allies. The militia was so brutal in victory, slaughtering captured horses and mutilating surrendering Natives, that the Army dismissed them immediately after the truce.

Below: **Alby and Hattie (Hatty) Shawaway, Yakima Indians, c. 1950, wearing beaded attire partly influenced by Plains Indians.**

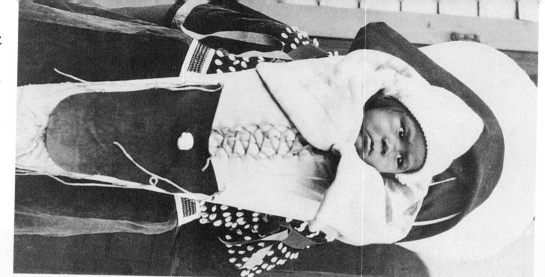

Above: Bannock mother and child, 1910, showing typical Basin/Plateau cradleboard. Although the mother is largely obscured, note her dress decorated with cowrie shells, and her beaded and brass-studded belt.

## BANNOCK

A branch separated from the Northern Paiute on the Snake River, Idaho, who became associated with the Northern Shoshone and in time intermixed. In culture they were similar to the Shoshone, and moved with them to the Fort Hall Reservation, Idaho, in 1869. In 1878, an Indian uprising in the area involved some Bannocks. In 1910, they numbered 413; and in 1945, 337. They are now mostly part of the "Shoshone-Bannock Tribe" of Fort Hall, Idaho, although Census 2000 reports 38 pure Bannock.

## CAYUSE

A tribe of the upper Walla Walla, Umatilla, and Grande Ronde rivers in northeastern Oregon, but originally from the Deschutes River area farther west. They are particularly famous for their horses. Some participated in the Whitman mission massacre of 1847, largely caused by disputes over land and fears about measles, which had killed 50% of one Cayuse band, and for which they blamed Dr. Whitman. Settled on the Umatilla Reservation, they numbered 404 in 1904, and 370 in 1937; but have largely merged into the "Confederated Umatilla," a composite of Umatilla, Walla Walla, and Cayuse. Census 2000 recorded only 60 Cayuse. The Cayuse language, together with the Molala (See Molala, page 53), formed a family called Waiilatpuan, thought to be distantly connected to the Sahaptians.

## CHELAN

A Salishan group on the west side of the Columbia, related to the Wenatchi; a few stayed until reservation days but seem to have joined the Wenatchi and Columbia (Sinkiuse) on the Colville Reservation.

## COEUR d'ALENE or SKITSWISH

The country occupied by this Salishan tribe was almost wholly within the present state of Idaho on the headwaters of the Spokane River, Coeur d'Alene Lake,

Above: **Cayuse man—note beadwork on shirt.**

below Lake Pend d'Oreille. Missionaries worked among them in the 1840s. The Coeur d'Alene Reservation in Benewah County, Idaho, was established in 1873, and has been home for most of their descendants since that time. They numbered 494 in 1905; 608 in 1937; 440 in 1970; and in Census 2000, 1,392 were recorded. They run the annual powwow at Worley.

## COLVILLE

A small Salishan tribe around Kettle Falls on the Columbia River, below the Canadian border in northeastern Washington, they became associated with the Hudson's Bay post at Fort Colville after its establishment in 1825. In 1872, the Colville Reservation was established on the western and northern sides of the Columbia, adjacent to the original domain, and the Colville have been there ever since, although now incorporated with many other tribes to form the modern "Confederated Tribes of the Colville Reservation." These tribes include the Sinkiuse or Columbia, Wenatchi, Chelan, Sanpoil, Nespelem, Okanagan, Lakes or Senijextee, and a few Nez Perce and Spokan. True Colville numbered 334 in 1907; Census 2000 reported 7,833. Rodeos and powwows are still held at Omak, Washington.

## KALISPEL

This Salishan tribe were also known as Pend d'Oreilles (hang ears), because of their large shell earrings. They were divided into the Upper Kalispel of western Montana, around Thompson Falls on the Pend d'Oreille River, and the Lower Kalispel extending into present northern Idaho up to Priest Lake, near the Canadian border. Like the Flatheads, they took part in the horse-bison culture, but their Plains traits were superficial. They were dominated by the fur trade and Catholic missionaries from the 1840s. Most of the Upper Kalispels and a few of the Lower Kalispels joined the Flatheads on the Flathead Reservation, numbering 640 and 197 respectively in 1905. The Lower Kalispels are also found on the Kalispel Reservation at Usk, Washington (est. 1914), and a few on the Colville Reservation. The Kalispel element of the combined confederated "Salish-

Below: **Klamath woman.**

Kutenai" are no longer reported alone, but the Kalispel Indian Community was recorded at 306 in Census 2000.

## KLAMATH

The Klamath lived in the area of rivers and marshes around Upper Klamath Lake, Oregon. They ceded their lands to the U.S. in 1864 and were given a reservation which they shared with the Modocs and some Paiutes. In time they became mixed with Euro-Americans and lost much of their culture, which led the Bureau of Indian Affairs to end the reservation's status and government programs and assistance. However, the tribe's descendants are pressing for new government recognition. In 1958, a total of 2,133 were enrolled—all the people of Klamath, Modoc, and Yahooskin Paiute descent living on and off their former reservation. Census 2000 reported 2,632 Klamaths. With the Modocs, their language formed a small family called Lutuamian, that was distantly related to the Sahaptians.

## KLICKITAT

This group lived along the Klickitat and White Salmon Rivers, Klickitat County, Washington. They were related closely to the Yakima groups but also intermarried with the Cowlitz to the west, and possibly numbered 600 in 1780. They were included in the Yakima Treaty of 1855 and moved to the Yakima Reservation, where they have merged over the years into the Yakima population (see pages 48–49). In 1910, 405 were reported separately; in 1970, only 21.

## LILLOOET (STL'ATL'IMX)

A large group of Salishan people on the Fraser River in British Columbia, around the town of Lillooet and Anderson Lake, the valley of Harrison Lake, and Lillooet Lake and River. Although historically similar to their relatives the Shuswap and Thompson, they lost more members in the smallpox epidemic of 1865. Their main reserves are at Douglas, Skookum Chuck, Lillooet, Bridge River, Anderson Lake, Fountain, Cayoose Creek, and Mount Currie. They numbered 2,494 in 1970.

Above: **Klickitat man.**

## METHOW

A small group on the Methow River in north central Washington. They joined the Columbia or Sinkiuse on the Colville Reservation (see page 51) and lost separate identity.

## MODOC

The southern branch of the Lutuamian family, they lived around the Lower Klamath, Tule, and Clear lakes in northern California. The Modocs are remembered for their stubborn resistance to American troops in the northern California Lava Beds in 1872 under their leader, Captain Jack. As a result, a number exiled to Indian Territory, although some returned. A few descendants remain in Oklahoma today. The majority of the Modocs were incorporated among the KlamathS on their reservation. Census 2000 recorded 478 Modoc, including 12 Oklahoma Modoc.

## MOLALA

This second branch of the Waiilatpuan family lived on the eastern slopes of the Cascade Range in central Oregon, and later on the Santiam and Molalla Rivers on the west side. The last of these people were said to be on the Grand Ronde Reservation, and a few may still be in the Lincoln County area of Oregon. The census of 1910 gave 31, but they are no longer separately reported. (See also Cayuse, page 50.)

## OKANAGAN or SINKAIETK

This Inland Salish tribe lived along the Okanagan River, Washington, and north into Canada on the Similkameen River and Lake Okanagan. Estimated to number 2,500 in around 1790, the Canadian bands settled on reserves around Lake Okanagan, at Okanagan, Westbank, Penticton, Upper and Lower Similkameen, and Osoyoos, numbering over 1,500 in 1970. A few southern Okanagan were enrolled at the Colville agency, numbering 187 in 1906. Their descendants are now part of the "Confederated Colville" (see page 51).

## PALOUSE

A group of Sahaptians occupying the Columbia River

## TRIBAL RIGHTS AND BUSINESSES TODAY

Many tribes today have re-secured their land rights through skilled litigation. A number have reclaimed their tribal status in order to take advantage of non-tax and other dispensations previously accorded to them through treaty. These often include gaming rights, allowing a number of tribes to invest in gaming operations that enrich their communities. Profits often go toward building hospitals, schools, and cultural centers and creating jobs that improve the standard of living for both Indians and the areas in which they live.

## SHAHAPTIAN OR SAHAPTIAN

A linguistic family restricted to the American Plateau area, including the Nez Perce, Yakima, Tenino, and others. Some think that this linguistic family is distantly related to the Klamath and Modoc, as well as to the Cayuse and Molala, but these connections are not wholly accepted.

*Below:* Nespelem (Nespilim) woman, c. 1907. The Nespelem were a small Interior Salish tribe related to the Sanpoil and Okanagan. Their descendants are now part of the many related groups called "Confederated Colville" of the Colville Reservation in Washington State.

valley above its junction with the Snake and along the Palouse River valley. They included the Chimnapum, Wanyukma, and Wanapum or Sokulks; the confusing term "Wanapam" has been added, but this is probably the same as Wanapam, the people who lived around Priest Rapids on the Columbia. Although included in the Yakima Treaty of 1855, only a few moved to various reservations, most choosing to remain in their homelands. As a result, few Palouse or Wanapum remain today. The Sahaptians were a village people with few political tribal organizations. On the whole, the Palouse's Plateau lifestyle involved wintertime occupancy of river villages and summertime camping at fishing and root-digging grounds. The Winter Guardian Spirit Dance was the major religious ceremony of such Plateau tribes. Smohalla, an Indian religious leader of the nineteenth century, was a Wanapum. A few descendants survive at Priest Rapids and other locations on the Columbia River.

## SALISHAN (INTERIOR)

The Salishan tribes of the mountains, valleys, and rivers of the Canadian Cordillera and the American Plateau regions, while linguistically connected to their kindred of the coast, were much different in culture. Their houses were conical mat lodges, sometimes extended to communal lodges, and semi-underground insulated winter dwellings. Like other Plateau Indians, their skills at fishing, basketry, making woven bags, and skin-dressing were well-developed. In later years they took on aspects of Plains culture and adopted the tipi, particularly the eastern groups such as the Flathead.

## SANPOIL & NESPELEM

Two closely related Salishan groups on the Sanpoil and Nespelem Rivers in north central Washington state. They made no treaty with the U.S. government, although ultimately most appear to have moved to the Colville Reservation. The Sanpoil numbered 202 in 1915 and the Nespelem 45 in 1910. The 1970 census reported 1,674 Sanpoil, Nespelem, Okanagan, and Spokan in the United States. The Sanpoil and Nespelem have now largely merged with the "Confederated Colville" (see page 51).

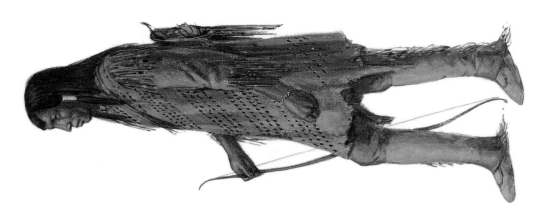

Below: Spokan man, c. 1846. Canadian artist Paul Kane traveled west across the interior, reaching Fort Vancouver in December 1846. Near Fort Colville, he painted an Indian with combined bow case and quiver, as well as a second bow, and wearing a pierced buckskin shirt imbued with protective power.

## SENIJEXTEE or LAKES

This Salishan tribe lived on the Columbia River north of Kettle Falls, Washington, and on the Kettle River into Canada to Lower Arrow Lake. Those on the south side of the international border joined the various tribes of the Colville Reservation (see page 51), being reported as 542 in 1909. Any north of the border are thought to have merged with the Okanagan.

## SHUSHWAP (SHUSWAP)

An important Salishan tribe living north of the Thompson Indians in British Columbia, from the vicinity of Ashcroft north to Williams Lake in the upper valleys of the Fraser River, and along the Thompson River above Kamloops, and also in the valley of the upper Columbia. Once numbering over 5,000 and known to the early explorers and later traders and miners, they never left their ancient homes, although they were restricted to small reserves, usually near old village sites. Their main groups are at Bonaparte, Ashcroft, Dead Man's Creek, Kamloops, Adams Lake, Pavilion, Spallumcheen, Clinton, North Thompson, Canoe Creek, Williams Lake, Alkali Lake, Canim Lake, and High Bar. Numbering 3,862 in 1970; some may still live around lake Okanagan today.

## SINKIUSE or COLUMBIA

A group of Salishan bands on the east side of the Columbia River from Fort Okanagan to Priest Rapids, Washington, where one band called Moses-Columbia lived. They were originally estimated to number 1,000; the census of 1910 reported only 52; and the 150 reported in 1959 largely merged with the "Confederated Colville" (see page 51) on the Colville Reservation. In 1970, 33 Columbia and Wenatchi were reported.

## SPOKANE

A Salishan tribe on the Spokane and Little Spokane rivers in eastern Washington, closely related to their eastern neighbors. They became associated with white traders after Spokane House was established in 1810, and were assigned to several reservations in the late nineteenth century, principally the Spokane Reservation, Wellpinit, Washington, and some with the Flathead in

Above: **Thompson River Salish woman;** of particular interest is the beaded and studded headband worn over the burden strap that supports her basket.

Montana, reported as 454 and 135, respectively, in 1910. In 1937, they reported 847, and in 1985, 1,961. Summer dances, games, and exhibits are still held at Wellpinit. Census 2000 recorded 2,198 Spokanes.

## TENINO

A group of Sahaptian bands and villages principally along the Deschutes and John Day Rivers, mainly on the south side of the Columbia River in Oregon, including the Tyigh, Tilkuni, Tukspush (or John Day Indians), and Waiim (or Wyam), to which can be added the Tapanash and Skinpah on the north side. Although a few seem to have gone to the Yakima Reservation, the majority, after the Wasco Treaty of 1855, moved to the Warm Springs Reservation, Oregon, where a merged Wasco-Tenino-Paiute population remains. In 1945, 544 Tenino were reported, plus a few John Days. In 1985, over 2,000 Warm Springs residents were enrolled. A few Waiams continued to occupy old fishing sites along the Columbia until recent times. Root feasts and powwows are still popular on the Warm Springs Reservation.

## THOMPSON or NTLAKYAPMUK

A large interior Salishan tribe living on the Fraser River, British Columbia, from Spuzzum in the south to above Lytton, then along the Thompson River to an area above Spencer Bridge, and east along the Nicola Valley. First noted by Simon Fraser in 1809, they subsequently came under the influence of the Northwest and Hudson's Bay traders. Although depleted during the nineteenth century, they continued to occupy village sites which became small reserves. The most important are Spuzzum, Boston Bar, Boothroyd, Kanaka Bar, Lytton, Oregon Jack Creek, and Upper and Lower Nicola. The total population numbered 2,742 in 1970.

## UMATILLA

The Umatillas lived on the lower Umatilla River near its junction with the Columbia in present Umatilla County, Oregon. Reported to number 1,500 in 1780, they had

Above: Umatilla mat lodge, c. 1860. Before they adopted Plains-type canvas tipis in the late nineteenth century, Plateau peoples used pole lodges covered with either cattail or tule mats, usually sewn but sometimes twined. The conical shape was only one of several ground plans, including rectangular, and parallel-sided with one or both ends rounded. The Yakima had a structure with vertical walls and gable roof resembling West Coast house shapes.

Below: Umatilla girl wearing a basket hat and earrings.

dwindled to a few hundred by the time of the Walla Walla Treaty of 1855, when they were assigned to the Umatilla Reservation along with the Walla Walla and Cayuse. They numbered 272 in 1910 and 161 in 1950, but they are a large element in the confederated "Umatilla," including the other groups, given as 1,234 in 1956; Census 2000 gives 1,549. They still hold root feasts, and participate in the powwows at the Pendleton Roundup each September.

## WALLAWALLA or WALULA

A group of Sahaptians on the Walla Walla River on the south side of the Snake near its junction with the Columbia, in southeastern Washington. Closely related to the Nez Perce, they were met by Lewis and Clark in 1805, and subsequently traders and trappers soon filtered into their domain. They moved to the Umatilla Reservation, Oregon, following the Walla Walla Treaty in 1855. Perhaps numbering over 1,000 in pre-reservation days, they reported as 397 in 1910 and 623 in 1945. They have now largely merged with the Cayuse and Umatilla and are known as the "Confederated Tribes of the Umatilla Reservation" (see above).

## WASCO

A Chinookan group, closely related to the Wishram (See *Native Tribes of the North and Northwest Coast* title in this series.)

## WISHRAM

A large Chinookan group, closely related to the Wishram, covered in our North and Northwest series title; today reported with the Yakima.

## WENATCHEE (WENATCHI) and ENTIAT

Two small Salishan groups on the west side of the Columbia River on the Wenatchee and Entiat Rivers around Leavenworth, Washington. Not all moved to the reservations, but some went to the Colville Reservation; these numbered 52 in 1910 and 268 in 1959, both on and off the reservation. They are now part of the "Confederated Colville" (see page 51).

GLOSSARY

**Agency.** Represents the federal government on one or more Indian reservations under the Bureau of Indian Affairs (BIA), which is headed by a presidentially appointed commissioner. Many agencies, especially in the nineteenth century, were corrupt and often took financial advantage of the Indians they were supposed to manage and support.

**Allotment.** Legal process, c. 1880s–1930s, by which land on reservations not allocated to Indian families was made available to whites.

**Anthropomorphic.** Having the shape or characteristics of humans; usually refers to an animal or god.

**Appliqué.** Decorative technique involving sewing quills (usually porcupine) and seed beads onto hide or cloth, using two threads, to create a flat mosaic surface.

**Apron.** Male apparel, front and back, which replaced the breechcloth for festive clothing during the nineteenth and twentieth centuries.

**Bandolier bag.** A prestige bag, with a shoulder strap, usually heavily beaded, worn by men and sometimes women at tribal dances, common among the Ojibwa and other Woodland groups.

**Birch bark.** Strong, thick bark used for canoes and various wigwam coverings as well as for a wide variety of containers that were adapted for the European souvenir trade by the addition of colored porcupine quills, such as those produced by the Mi'kmaq and by the Ojibwa and Odawa of the Great Lakes area.

**Buckskin.** Hide leather from animals of the deer family—deer (white-tailed deer in the East, mule deer in the West), moose, or elk—used for clothing. The hides of buffalo, bighorn sheep, Dall sheep, mountain goat, and caribou were less commonly used.

**Bureau of Indian Affairs (BIA).** Begun in 1824, transferred from

**58** NATIVE TRIBES OF THE GREAT BASIN AND PLATEAU

the War Department to the Department of the Interior in 1849. Now, around half of the BIA's employees are Native American, and the Bureau provides services through its agencies in many big cities as well as on rural reservations.

**Confederacy.** A group of peoples or villages bound together politically or for defense (e.g., Iroquois, Creek).

**Cradles.** Any of three main devices used across the continent to transport or carry babies: the cradle board of the Woodland tribes (cloth or skin attached to a wooden board with a protecting angled bow), the baby-carrier of the Plains (a bag on a frame or triangular hood with a cloth base folded around the baby), and the flat elliptical board covered with skin or cloth, with a shallow bag or hide straps, of the Plateau.

**Drum or Dream Dance.** A variation of the Plains Grass Dance adopted by the Santee Sioux, Chippewa (Ojibwa or Ojibwe), and Menominee during the nineteenth century. Among these groups the movement had religious features that advocated friendship, even with whites.

**Ethnographer.** An anthropologist who studies and describes individual cultures.

**Hairpipes.** Tubular bone beads made by whites and traded to the Indians, often made up into vertical and horizontal rows called breastplates.

**Lazy stitch.** A Plains technique of sewing beads to hide or cloth, giving a final ridged or arch effect in lanes about eight or ten beads wide.

**Leggings.** Male or female, covering ankle and leg to the knee or thigh (male), usually buckskin or cloth.

**Longhouse.** The religion of conservative Iroquois, whose rituals still take place in special buildings also called longhouses.

**Medicine bundle.** A group of objects, sometimes animal, bird,

or mineral, contained in a wrapping of buckskin or cloth, that gave access to considerable spiritual power when opened with the appropriate ritual. Mostly found among the eastern and Plains groups.

**Moiety.** A ceremonial division of a village, tribe, or nation.

**Pan-Indian.** A description of the modern mixed intertribal dances, costumes, powwows, and socializing leading to the reinforcement of ethnic and nationalist ties.

**Parfleche.** A rawhide envelope or box made to contain clothes or meat, often decorated with painted geometrical designs.

**Peyote.** A stimulant and hallucinogenic substance obtained from the peyote buttons of the mescal cactus.

**Peyote Religion.** The Native American Church, a part-native and part-Christian religion originating in Mexico but developed among the Southern Plains tribes in Oklahoma, which has spread to many Native communities.

**Powwow.** Modern celebration, often intertribal and secular, held on most reservations throughout the year.

**Prehistoric.** In a Eurocentric view of American Indian archaeology, Indian life and its remains dated before A.D. 1492.

**Rancherias** Small reservations in California.

**Rawhide.** Usually hard, dehaired hide or skin used for parfleche cases, moccasin soles, shields, and drum-heads.

**Reservation.** Government-created lands to which Indian peoples were assigned, removed, or restricted during the nineteenth and twentieth centuries. In Canada they are called reserves.

**Roach.** A headdress of deer and porcupine hair, very popular for male war-dance attire, which

originated among the eastern tribes and later spread among the Plains Indians along with the popular Omaha or Grass Dance, the forerunner of the modern War and Straight dances.

**Sinew.** The tendon fiber from animals, used as thread for sewing purposes.

**Sweat lodge.** A low, temporary, oval-shaped structure covered with skins or blankets, in which one sits in steam produced by splashing water on heated stones as a method of ritual purification.

**Syllabics.** A form of European-inspired writing consisting of syllabic characters used by the Cherokee in the nineteenth century and in other forms by the Cree and Inuit.

**Termination.** Withdrawal of U.S. government recognition of the protected status of, and services due to, an Indian reservation.

**Tipi.** Bags, usually buckskin, used for storage inside tipis.

**Tobacco or pipe bag.** Cases for men to carry ceremonial tobacco and pipes, usually made of buckskin that is beaded or quilled with fringing, made by most Plains peoples.

**Tribe.** A group of bands linked together genetically, politically, geographically, by religion, by a common origin myth, or, most often, by a common language. The term "Tribe" often arouses controversy: Many prefer "Nation" or "People." Ethnographers often use the word to describe people in fragmented or small groups who themselves recognize no such association.

**War dance.** Popular name for the secular male dances developed in Oklahoma and other places after the spread of the Grass Dances from the eastern Plains-Prairie tribes, among whom it was connected with war societies. Many tribes had complex war and victory celebrations.

# MUSEUMS & FURTHER READING

## MUSEUMS

The United States naturally has the largest number of museums, with vast holdings of Indian material and art objects. The most important was that of George Heye, whose Peabody Museum of Archaeology and Ethnology at Harvard University, in Cambridge, Massachusetts, has over 500,000 ethnographic objects pertaining to North America, including a large number of Northwest Coast pieces. Many collections of Indian artifacts in major U.S. institutions were assembled by ethnologists and archaeologists who were working for, or contracted to, various major museums, such as Frank Speck and Frances Densmore for the Smithsonian Institution, Washington, D.C., or George Dorsey for the Field Museum of Natural History, Chicago.

Since the sixteenth century, the material culture of the Native peoples of North America has been collected and dispersed around the world. These objects, where they survived, often found their way into European museums, some founded in the eighteenth century. Unfortunately, these objects usually have missing or incomplete documentation, and because such material was collected during the European (British, French, Spanish, Russian) and later American exploration, exploitation, and colonization of North America, these collections may or may not accurately represent Native cultures. Collectors in the early days were usually sailors (Captain Cook), soldiers (Sir John Caldwell), Hudson's Bay Company agents, missionaries, traders, or explorers.

During the twentieth century, a number of museums have developed around the collections of private individuals. The most important was that of George Heye, whose museum was founded in 1916 (opened 1922) and located in New York City. It was called the Museum of the American Indian, Heye Foundation. This collection has now been incorporated into the National Museum of the American Indian, a huge building sited on the Mall in Washington, D.C., scheduled to open in September 2004. Other notable privately owned collections subsequently purchased or presented to scholarly institutions are the Haffenreffer Museum Collection at Brown University, Rhode Island; much of Milford G. Chandler's collection, which is now at the Detroit Institute of Arts; Adolph Spohr's collection at the Buffalo Bill Historical Center, Cody, Wyoming; and the impressive Arthur Speyer collection at the National Museums of Canada, Ottawa.

Many U.S. and Canadian museums and institutions have been active in publishing popular and scholarly ethnographic reports, including the Glenbow-Alberta Institute, the Royal Ontario Museum, Toronto, and, pre-eminently, the Smithsonian Institution, Washington, D.C. Most of the major U.S. museums have organized significant exhibitions of Indian art, and their accompanying catalogs and publications, often with Native input, contain important and valuable information.

In the recent past, a number of Indian-owned and -run museums have come into prominence, such as the Seneca-Iroquois National Museum, Salamanca, New York; the Turtle Museum at Niagara Falls; Woodland Cultural Centre, Brantford, Ontario, Canada; and the Pequot Museum, initiated with funding from the Pequots' successful gaming operation in Connecticut. The Pequots have also sponsored a number of Indian art exhibitions. Many smaller tribal museums are now found on a number of reservations across the United States.

There has also been much comment, debate, and honest disagreement between academics (Indian and non-Indian alike), museum personnel, and historians about the role of museums and the validity of ownership of Indian cultural material in what have been, in the past, non-Native institutions. Certain Indian groups have, through the legal process, won back from museums a number of funerary and religious objects, where these have been shown to be of major importance to living tribes or nations. The Native American Graves and Repatriation Act of 1990, now a federal law, has guided institutions to return artifacts to Native petitioners; some, such as the Field Museum of Chicago, while not strictly bound by this law, have voluntarily returned some remains and continue to negotiate loans and exchanges with various Native American groups. A listing of U.S. museums with Native American resources may be found at http://www.hanksville.org/NAresources/indices/NAmuseums.html.

## FURTHER READING

Birchfield, D. L.( General Ed.): *The Encyclopedia of North American Indians,* Marshall Cavendish, 1997.

Brody, H.: *Maps and Dreams,* Jill Norman and Hobhouse Ltd., 1981.

Bruchac, Joseph: *Journal of Jesse Smoke: A Cherokee Boy, Trail of Tears, 1838.* Scholastic, Inc., 2001.

Buller, Laura: *Native Americans: An Inside Look at the Tribes and Traditions,* DK Publishing, Inc., 2001.

Coe, R. T.: *Sacred Circles: Two Thousand Years of North American Indian Art;* Arts Council of GB, 1976.

Cooper, Michael J.: *Indian School: Teaching the White Man's Way,* Houghton Mifflin Company, 1999.

Davis, M. B. (Ed.): *Native America in the Twentieth Century;* Garland Publishing, Inc., 1994.

Dennis, Y. W., Hirschfelder, A. B., and Hirschfelder, Y.: *Children of Native America Today,* Charlesbridge Publishing, Inc., 2003.

Despard, Yvone: *Folk Art Projects - North America,* Evan-Moor Educational Publishers, 1999.

Downs, D.: *Art of the Florida Seminole and Miccosukee Indians,* University Press of Florida, 1995.

Duncan, K. C.: *Northern Athapaskan Art: A Beadwork Tradition,* Un. Washington Press, 1984.

Ewers, J. C.: *Blackfeet Crafts,* "Indian Handicraft" series; Educational Division, U.S. Bureau of Indian Affairs, Haskell Institute, 1944.

Fenton, W. N.: *The False Faces of the Iroquois,* Un. Oklahoma Press, 1987.

Fleming, P. R., and Luskey, J.: *The North American Indians in Early Photographs,* Dorset Press, 1988.

Frazier, P: *The Mohicans of Stockbridge,* Un. Nebraska Press, Lincoln, 1992.

Gidmark, D.: *Birchbark Canoe, Living Among the Algonquin,* Firefly Books, 1997.

Hail, B. A., and Duncan, K. C.: *Out of the North: The Subarctic Collection of the Haffenreffer Museum of Anthropology,* Brown University, 1989.

Harrison, J. D.: *Métis: People Between Two Worlds,* The Glenbow-Alberta Institute in association with Douglas and McIntyre, 1985.

Hodge, F. (Ed.): *Handbook of American Indians North of Mexico,* two vols, BAEB 30; Smithsonian Institution, 1907–10.

Howard, J. H.: *Reprints in Anthropology Vol. 20:The Dakota or Sioux Indians,* J and L Reprint Co., 1980.

——: *Shawnee: The Ceremonialism of a Native American Tribe and its Cultural Background,* Ohio University Press, 1981.

Huck, B.: *Explaining the Fur Trade Routes of North America,* Heartland Press, 2000.

Johnson, M. J.: *Tribes of the Iroquois Confederacy,* "Men at Arms" series No. 395; Osprey Publishing, Ltd, 2003.

King, J. C. H.: *Thunderbird and Lightning: Indian Life in Northeastern North America 1600–1900,* British Museum Publications Ltd., 1982.

Lake-Thom, Bobby: *Spirits of the Earth: A Guide to Native American Symbols, Stories and Ceremonies,* Plume, 1997.

Lyford, C. A.: *The Crafts of the Ojibwa,* "Indian Handicrafts" series, U.S. BIA 1943.

Page, Jack: *In the Hands of the Great Spirit: The 20,000 Year History of American Indians,*The Free Press, 2003.

Paredes, J. A. (Ed.): *Indians of the Southwestern U.S. in the late 20th Century,* Un. Alabama Press, 1992.

Press, Petra, and Sita, Lisa: *Indians of the Northwest: Traditions, History, Legends and Life,* Gareth Stevens, 2000.

Rinaldi, Anne, *My Heart Is on the Ground: The Diary of Nannie Little Rose, a Sioux Girl, Carlisle Indian School, Pennsylvania, 1880* (Dear American Series), Scholastic Inc., 1999.

Scriver, B.: *The Blackfeet: Artists of the Northern Plains,* The Lowell Press Inc., 1990.

Sita, Lisa: *Indians of the Northeast: Traditions, History, Legends and Life,* Gareth Stevens, 2000.

——: *Indians of the Great Plains: Traditions, History, Legends and Life,* Gareth Stevens, 2000.

——: *Indians of the Southwest: Traditions, History, Legends and Life,* Gareth Stevens, 2000.

Swanton, John R.: *Indian Tribes of the Lower Mississippi Valley and Adjacent Coast of the Gulf of Mexico;* BAEB 43; Smithsonian Institution, 1911. *Early History of the Creek Indians and Their Neighbors;* BAEB 73; Smithsonian Institution, 1922. ——: *Indians of the Southeastern United States;* BAEB 137; Smithsonian Institution, 1946.

—— *The Indian Tribes of North America;* BAEB 145; Smithsonian Institution, 1952.

Waldman, Carl: *Atlas of The North American Indian,* Checkmark Books, 2000.

Wright, Muriel H.: *A Guide to the Indian Tribes of Oklahoma,* Un. Oklahoma Press, 1951.

**59** MUSEUMS AND FURTHER READING

This index cites references to all six volumes of the Native Tribes of North America set, using the following abbreviations for each of the books: GB = Great Basin and Plateau, NE = Northeast, NW = North and Northwest Coast, PP = Plains and Prairie, SE = Southeast, SW = California and the Southwest.

## ABOUT THE CONTRIBUTORS

**Dr. Duncan Clarke (Contributing Author)**
Clarke has a master's degree from London University's School of Oriental and African Studies and has recently completed his PhD., focusing on the history of textiles in the Yoruba region of Nigeria. He is currently working as a freelance writer and lecturer on ethnic art and as a dealer in antique textiles.

**Richard Hook (Illustrator and Contributing Author)**
An internationally respected professional illustrator specializing in historical and anthropological subjects for more than thirty years, Hook has had a lifelong interest in Native American culture that has inspired his remarkable artwork. He has been widely published in the United States, Europe, and Japan. A lifelong interest in Native American culture led to his selection as illustrator for the Denali Press Award-winning The Encyclopedia of Native American Tribes.

**Michael G. Johnson (Author)**
Johnson has researched the material culture, demography, and linguistic relationships of many Native American peoples for more than thirty years, through academic institutions in North America and Europe and during numerous field studies conducted with the cooperation and hospitality of many Native American communities. He has published a number of books, in particular the Denali Press Award-winning Encyclopedia of Native American Tribes.